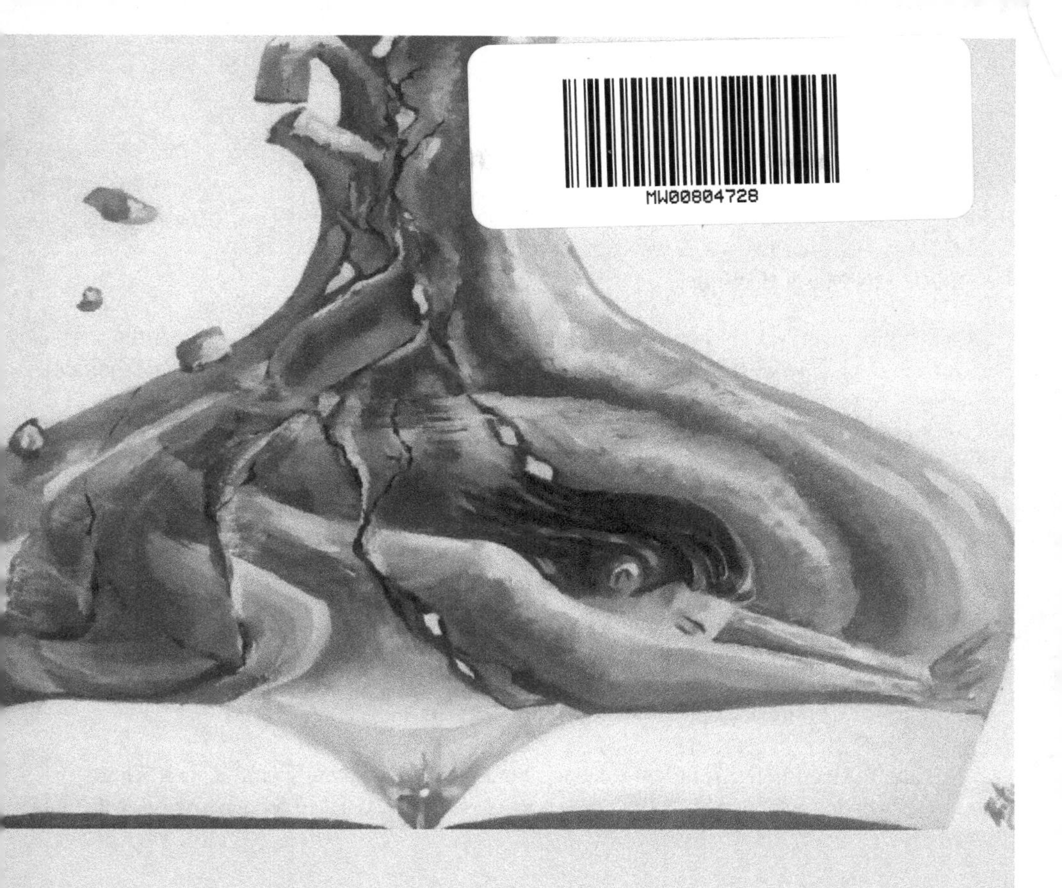

Chosen Vessels Pray With Purpose and Passion

Praying and Journaling Psalms and Proverbs

MARIA E. WHITE

Gifted Publishing

Chosen Vessels Pray with Purpose and Passion

Requests for information should be addressed to:

Gifted Publishing
www.giftedpublishing.com

ISBN: 978-1-7358977-0-7 paperback
ISBN: 978-1-7358977-1-4 eBook

Library of Congress Control Number: 2020921855

Artist for Cover Design: Portia Sampson
Editor: Angie Zachary
Book Layout Designer: Dahlia Marcano
Author's Photo, Photographer: Reginald White

Printed in the United States of America

DEDICATION

This prayer devotional consists of a book of inspirational thoughts. *Chosen Vessels Pray with Purpose and Passion* is dedicated to the women who faithfully, for two and a half years, offered prayers, words of inspiration, and exhortation to other women on Monday evenings at 9:01 p.m. The time together caused a prayer movement amongst wives, sisters, cousins, and friends.

It is my prayer that these inspirational words will offer help to God's Chosen Vessels, especially wives, their families, and friends to have a more intimate relationship with God. From these prayers, I want humanity to reflect on God's Word daily and use this resource as an opportunity to pray Scriptures to affect life situations and circumstances. I also want to encourage readers to create songs of praise during their quiet time with God.

A question that may come to mind is, *What is prayer?* Prayer is transformative. I like this acronym for prayer that God gave me over twenty years ago:

Purpose

Revealed

Always *when you*

Yield to the everlasting Father *and*

Establish *a*

Relationship with *Him, our Lord, Savior, and God.*

Remember, Chosen Vessels pray daily and relationships matter to God!

Chosen *(selected and appointed)*

Vessels *(containers, carriers, or a place to hold things)*

Pray *(corporate or individual conversation with God daily)*

Throughout your journey, through selected chapters in the Book of Psalms and selected chapters in Proverbs, God will infuse His Word into your life. You will glean how your life should offer true worship to Abba Father, which art in heaven.

As you reflect on the Scripture selections and the questions of the day related to Psalms and Proverbs, take time to reflect, give praise and worship, and recommit to applying God's Word to every situation in your life. Use this time to open your heart, soul, and mind as you reflect on the benefits of praising God in every situation, and know God's Word will empower you with the wisdom of God so you can access His grace, mercy, and love continually.

Therefore, ***Chosen Vessels***, let us enter boldly into God's presence and embrace His anointing by…

† Finding your purpose for the day,

† Allowing God's passion to be at the helm of your life,

† Commit to persevering no matter what you meet throughout the day.

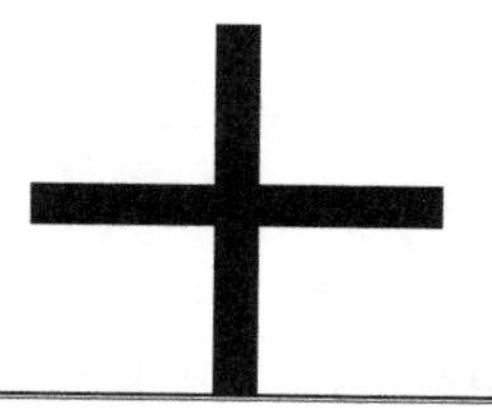

"Each time, before you intercede, be quiet first and worship God in His glory. Think of what He can do, and how He delights to the prayers of His redeemed people. Think of your place and privilege in Christ, and expect great things!" **– Andrew Murray**

ACKNOWLEDGEMENTS / NOTES

Let us gather like the geese and graze on God's Word as we taste and see that God is good! For it is written in Ezekiel 34:14 (NKJV),

> "I will feed them in good pasture, and their fold [grazing ground] shall be on the high mountain of Israel. There they shall lie down on good fold [grazing ground] and feed in rich pasture on the mountains of Israel."

To *God*: I extend a heartfelt thanks for inspiring me to graze on Your Word and finishing my assignment in authoring this book.

To *Reginald*: I am grateful that you are my suitable lovable partner.

To *Reginald, Jaleea* [daughter-in-love], *Ryan Joshua* [grandson], and *Ramar*: I love each of you beyond measure.

To *Edmond and Earlis Stamps*: You gave me life, taught me to pray with purpose, and instilled in me to lead as your firstborn. I praise God for your wisdom and unwavering faith.

To *Marian, Edmond II, Michelle, and Marshan*: We are mighty because we are a **F**amily **I**nspired **S**tanding **S**trong **T**ogether (the **FISST**). I am grateful to be your big sister.

To *my church family (First Baptist Church of Glenarden)*: Words cannot express my gratitude. My life has been so blessed by the Word shared with my family and me. *A special thanks to Pastor John K. Jenkins, Sr, First Lady Trina E. Jenkins [Family Life Ministries, Department Head], Mother Geneva Pearson, founder and former director of Wives' Support Ministry, and Jackie Parker, Director, Women's Focus Study* who sowed into my leadership and mentored me.

To *Portia Sampson*: I am grateful that you captured my vision and provided me your artistic expression of a posture of prayer for a Chosen Vessel. I appreciate your giftings and love you!

To *Angie Zachary*: Thank you for helping me to share my thoughts, know I value you as my "*editor*" and I appreciate you!

To *Dahlia Marcano*: Thank you for your creative style and typesetting skills. I value you as my *book layout designer* and I appreciate you!

To my "*proofreaders*": Paula B. Bellamy, Tonya Johnson-Hunter, Kendra Evans, The Stamps-Berry Family, Jaleea White, and Imani Coley. Thank you for helping me and know I appreciate you!

To *Dr. Celeste*: I am so grateful that you were my wise book doula whose blogging, podcasting, and self-publishing tips helped me to publish this book. May the Lord bless the Dr. Celeste Owens Ministries.

To Beth: Thank you for the inspiration, encouragement, and your publishing expertise. May God continue to bless Inspire-Books.

To my *motivation prayer crew*: Robin, Dellecia, Chae, and the 1,000 plus *Chosen Vessels Pray Conference Call* Callers, who helped me so much to complete this assignment.

Notes

Merriam Webster Dictionary (10th ed.). (1999).

1. Blessed, p. 1
2. Prospects, p. 73
3. Revive, p. 80
4. If, p. 112
5. Beauty, p. 153
6. Avails, p. 181
7. Wellspring, p. 213

CONTENTS

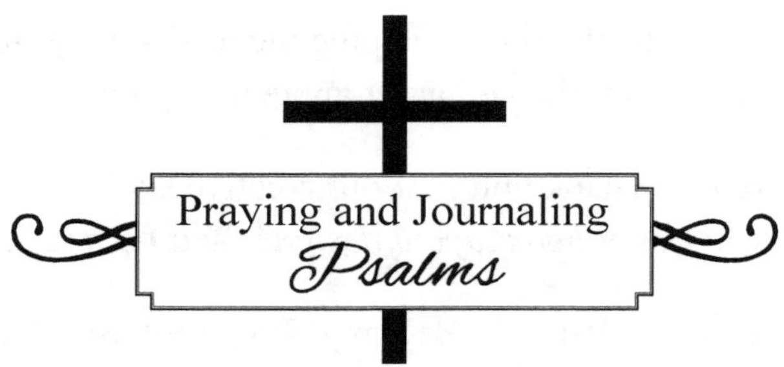

Prayer Themes

Prayer Themes

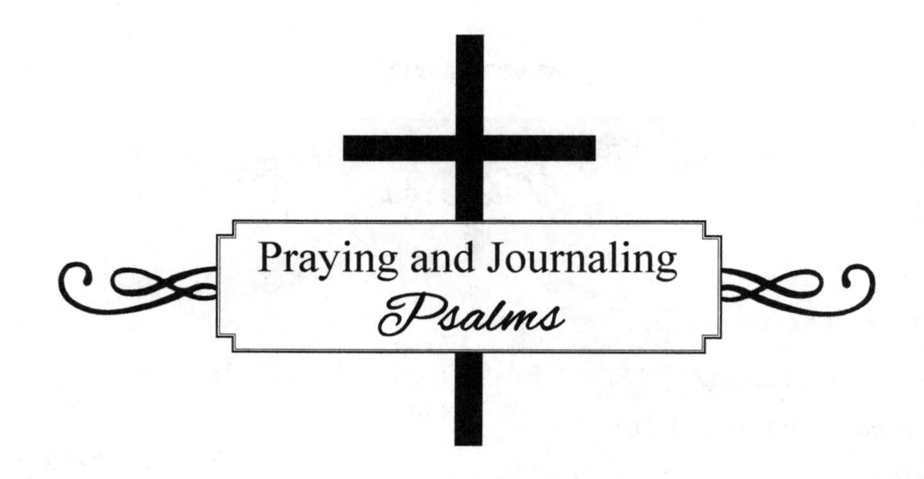
Praying and Journaling
Psalms

PRAYER THEME

Meditate and Be Planted

Prayer Focus: Psalm 1:1-3, NKJV

Blessed *is* the man Who walks not in the counsel of the ungodly, Nor stands in the path of sinners, Nor sits in the seat of the scornful; But his delight *is* in the law of the LORD, And in His law he meditates day and night. He shall be like a tree Planted by the rivers of water, That brings forth its fruit in its season, Whose leaf also shall not wither; And whatever he does shall prosper.

Prayer Focus Reflection

Life brings seasons of change, but we can reflect on our giftings with one constant consolation: God is consistent, and He changes not. In Psalm 1, the Lord gives us an opportunity to worship, meditate, and sing praises unto Him. He teaches us that a lifestyle pleasing to Him offers blessing, honor, and hope. Through His Word, our God gives us instructions for life and lets us know the power of a blessed walk with Him.

To me, *blessed* means *favor and honor.* However, according to the *Merriam Webster Dictionary*, blessed is *being connected*. Therefore, Chosen Vessels, we are connected to favor and honor when we are rooted, grounded, and connected to God and His Word. As you walk this journey of life, set your roots in God's Word, meditate on His precepts day and night, and get relentlessly rooted and grounded as you take the principles of God's Word and plant them deeply in the heart of your soul. When you are grounded, your fruit shall ripen and spring forth.

What has God revealed to you as you meditate on the scripture?

Journal

QUESTIONS TO PONDER

Meditate and Be Planted

1. Have you considered God's purpose for your life today?
2. What passions lie inside you that have gone untapped?
3. Are you willing to persevere and go the distance, no matter what?

Let us pray:

Father help us to take some time today to connect to our ***purpose*** *and* **passion** *by* ***persevering****, no matter what. In Your name, Jesus, we pray, Amen.*

What is your prayer today?

Journal

Thankful for the Chosen One

Prayer Focus: Psalm 2:1-3, NKJV

Why do the nations rage, And the people plot a vain thing? The kings of the earth set themselves, And the rulers take counsel together, Against the LORD and against His Anointed, *saying*, "Let us break Their bonds in pieces, And cast away Their cords from us."

Prayer Focus Reflection

Today's prayer focus is on being thankful that Jesus Christ is the Chosen One. Give voice to thoughts of praise and adoration unto God. Allow God's Word to break all the plots that the enemy seeks to use to plague your heart and spirit. Our emotions can overwhelm us but having a godly attitude can help us during those darkest moments of life. In Psalms, David shares his pit experiences as well as his joyful or highest mountaintop experiences. He uses words that serve as prayers that one can journal and songs that bring forth a graceful praise unto Abba, Father who art in heaven. Throughout this Psalm, one can gain wisdom and deeper insight on how to live a godly life as a wise Chosen Vessel.

Let us be thankful and offer spiritual songs of praise unto God that will lift our hearts toward Him. Therefore, today we are thankful to God for:

- † giving us the support of family and friends.
- † giving us His Word, which enables us to be planted, rooted, and grounded.
- † giving us His steadiness, so we can remain connected to Him as the Vinedresser.
- † being our breath of life.
- † enabling us to grow in Him during personal struggles.
- † taking us through seasons of "less" while giving us more through His grace, mercy, love, and compassion.
- † strategically connecting us to "accountability partners."
- † enabling us to walk this spiritual journey.

Let us pray and give thanks unto the Lord:

Abba, Father, we thank You for Your Word and know that You enable us to bear good fruit for Your glory. We can sing aloud as in Isaiah 6:3b (NKJV), "Holy, holy, holy is the Lord of hosts; The whole earth is full of His glory!" Thank you for being a God who reigns.

God is sovereign over the nations and the ruler of the world, and He gave us His only begotten Son (John 3:16, NKJV), Jesus Christ, as the Chosen One for us. He came so that we can have eternal life. He came so that we can always remember that He is with us and will never leave us nor forsake us. He came so that we can help others learn of the gift of love that sacrificed His life for our liberty.

Through His sacrificed life, He gave us liberty. He changed our lives. He made us whole. Are you thankful for the love of God and the sacrificial Lamb He gave on our behalf? The price paid at Calvary mandates that everyone falls under the authority of God and everyone must answer to Him as Scripture tells us: Jesus Christ is Lord, and every knee will bow and every tongue shall confess to God (Romans 14:11, NKJV).

Therefore, Chosen Vessels, God is the only one who has authority over any situation we may encounter. Submitting to God grants us liberty; Jesus sacrificed His life for our liberty (freedom). Let us do as Psalm 2:11a (NKJV) says, "Serve the LORD," as well as Psalm 2:12b (NKJV) "Put [your] trust in Him." I guarantee that when you serve, honor, and trust God, provision, hope, peace, grace, mercy, love, and understanding shall prevail in abundance in your life, and you will be bonded to Him by His love.

What has God revealed to you as you meditate on the scripture?

____

____

____

____

____

____

____

____

____

____

____

____

____

____

______________________________ *Journal*

QUESTIONS TO PONDER

Thankful for the Chosen One

1. Have you considered God's purpose for your being thankful?
2. What passionate bond lies within you during those darkest moments?
3. Are you willing to go deeper to gain godly wisdom no matter what?

What is your prayer today?

Journal

PRAYER THEME

Consider My Meditation

Prayer Focus: Psalm 5:1-3, NKJV

Give ear to my words, O LORD, Consider my meditation. Give heed to the voice of my cry, My King and my God, For to You I will pray. My voice You shall hear in the morning, O LORD; In the morning I will direct *it* to You, And I will look up.

Prayer Focus Reflection

As you arise today, ask God to consider your words. Ask Abba to guide you throughout the day. You know God honors Vessels who carry His Word in their hearts. As you ponder on today's Scripture, select a few words, and cover your family and your situation. God's Word, love, and grace changes not, so follow the biblical principles offered in this passage of Scripture.

Rise early in the morning to meditate, Chosen Vessels, and spend some time seeking God. Be His Chosen Vessel who allows God to fill you up as His container of love, grace, and mercy to influence all whom you meet.

QUESTIONS TO PONDER

Consider My Meditation

1. Have you given ear to God's words today?
2. What passions lie inside you that have gone untapped?
3. Are you willing to follow the biblical principles offered in today's prayer focus?

Let us pray:

Dear Lord consider the meditation of our hearts this day. Help us Lord to heed to Your voice in every decision and relationship that we meet in the days ahead. Help us Lord to think before we speak and be Chosen Vessels who walk in love, peace, joy, and abide in Your love.

What is your prayer today?

Journal

PRAYER THEME

Consider God's Glory

Prayer Focus: Psalm 8:1-3, NKJV

O LORD, our Lord, How excellent *is* Your name in all the earth, Who have set Your glory above the heavens! Out of the mouth of babes and nursing infants, You have ordained strength, Because of Your enemies, That You may silence the enemy and the avenger. When I consider Your heavens, the work of Your fingers, The moon and the stars, which You have ordained.

Prayer Focus Reflection

Have you looked toward the heavens and begun to converse with God about how thankful you are for His creating the heavens and the earth? Well, Chosen Vessels, God's glory is magnificent, and today will be magnificent to you too. Throughout today, reflect on God's creation. Think about the magnificent things that He has done, especially for you, throughout the past few days before you began reading *Chosen Vessels Pray with Purpose and Passion.*

Is not it a blessing that God chose you, but He allows you to honor His choice and willingly obey and serve Him? Being formed by God, being granted the freedom to choose to serve Him, and being given the opportunity to experience His grace is so awesome. My choice is to serve God, every second and every minute of my life, and every day. What about you?

QUESTIONS TO PONDER

Consider God's Glory

1. Have you considered God's blessing for choosing you?
2. What passions lie inside you that may silence the enemy?
3. Are you willing to obey God and serve him no matter what?

What is your prayer today?

Journal

Acrostic Prayers of Thanksgiving

Prayer Focus: Psalm 9:1-3, NKJV

I will praise *You*, O Lord, with my whole heart; I will tell of all Your marvelous works. I will be glad and rejoice in You; I will sing praise to Your name, O Most High. When my enemies turn back, They shall fall and perish at Your presence.

Prayer Focus Reflection

Today's prayer focus is on God being the Righteous Judge of one's conduct. God's righteousness flows from His very character, and His character is the final standard of what is right and wrong (Psalms 9:5). This Psalm teaches us that God will take care of us in any situation and at His appointed time. In this Psalm, a Hebrew acrostic alphabet, which has 22 letters, serves as an aid in sharing God's goodness from A to Z.

As you read the Scripture aloud, you gave voice to an alphabet that stands for your personal testament to what the Scripture speaks to you. Today's acrostic words speak of God's greatness through this prayer:

Lord, we declare that You are the God of our lives. We declare to share with others Your goodness. We declare Your goodness over life situations and circumstances. We declare that You are the judge, and You have the final say. No matter what others say or do, You have the final word. Your judgment, Lord, is better than anything is. Even when we are reprimanded, we can still experience Your righteousness over our lives. Lord, You are the Lord of all, and You put our family, our friends, and our foes in fear, in reverence unto You. Father, nations may know themselves to be but men, but we reflect our dependency and need of You.

Most High, we wish to dwell daily in Your secret place. We rest in You, dear Lord, and we want to worship You in spirit and in truth. You, O God, are our refuge, and You change not. You are our strength. We love You for Your faithfulness and continual love toward us. Jehovah, we trust in You and know that by putting our confidence in You, we can experience Your sovereignty; and by trusting You, we are daily surrendering and submitting to Your will.

Abba, we can rejoice in You because You are the God of all battles. We thank You for Your Word and know that You, Lord, shall judge the world in righteousness and shall administer judgment. Father, we bless You for Your marvelous works to the children of men. We thank You for a memory of knowing where You brought us from and where You are taking us to. We thank You for Your mercy and giving us daily opportunities to meditate on Your Word day and night. We thank You that You, O Lord, "maintained [our] right and [our] cause." We want to continue to be Your beacons of light who declare the mighty acts of our Most High God, who joyfully take refuge and strength from Your Word, who respect Your righteous and Your judgment as the Lord of lords, and King of kings. We trust You, dear Lord, and we shall daily rejoice and sing praises unto Your name, Lord God, amen!

Therefore, Chosen Vessels, God is the only one who has authority over any situation we may encounter. Let us continue to praise God for His mercy and let God arise in our lives.

QUESTIONS TO PONDER

Acrostic Prayers of Thanksgiving

1. Have you considered your personal testament to being thankful?
2. What declarations do you need to make today?
3. Are you willing to thank God and tell others of His miraculous works?

What is your prayer today?

Journal

PRAYER THEME

Faithful and Righteous

Prayer Focus: Psalm 11:1-3, NKJV

In the LORD, I put my trust; How can you say to my soul, "Flee *as* a bird to your mountain"? For look! The wicked bend *their* bow; They make ready their arrow on the string, That they may shoot secretly at the upright in heart. If the foundations are destroyed, What can the righteous do?

Prayer Focus Reflection

In looking at the last part of Psalm 11:3, can God consider you righteous? Righteous is being in right standing with His principles of life. Throughout today, reflect on the benefits of being faithful and the benefits you receive throughout your life as you trust God. Think about how having an upright heart diverts arrows shot to devour you because God gives protection to the upright.

Yes, there will be times when the arrows of life will pierce your very soul. However, you can stand on God's Word and know that He will be with you, and that He will never leave you.

QUESTIONS TO PONDER

Faithful and Righteous

1. Have you allowed the arrows of life to change God's purposes that lie in you?
2. Have these arrows caused the passions that burn within you to become ashes?
3. Are you willing to persevere and allow God to make beauty from your ashes?

Let us pray:

Dear Lord, we ask You to stifle the arrows set out to harm us. Shield us and help us to walk upright and always remember that You dear Lord are always near us.

What is your prayer today?

___

___

___

___

___

___

___

___

___

___

___ *Journal*

PRAYER THEME

A Life Centered on the Lord

Prayer Focus: Psalm 16:1-3, NKJV

Preserve me, O God, for in You I put my trust. *O my soul*, you have said to the Lord, "You *are* my Lord, My goodness is nothing apart from You." As for the saints who *are* on the earth, "They are the excellent ones, in whom is all my delight."

Prayer Focus Reflection

Today's prayer focuses on keeping God at the center of your life, be it at home, in the workplace, or during any relationship. Psalm 16 speaks and echoes God's grace and mercy available to us. In addition, it focuses on the benefits we receive by having integrity as a Godly characteristic. This Psalm teaches us that by us adhering our lives and fully committing ourselves to God, we can take confidence in knowing that God will take care of us always, at all events, and in all circumstances!

As you read the Scripture aloud, you give voice to God mending your relationships and restoring your joy. Today allow this deeper understanding of the power of God's Word to launch you into the deeper things of God. Reflect on Psalm 16 as it prepares us for understanding the Lord's return. As you reflect on Psalm 16:2, 4, 5, 7, 9 and 11, begin to thank the Lord for His promises to us when we honor and trust Him. Write down the English word, then look up the Hebrew word and write down a prayer of thanks unto the Lord.

God gives us counsel or resolve (Hebrew word). He tells us that His goodness (Hebrew words for goodness are beautiful, best, better, bountiful, cheerful, at ease, favor, fine, gracious, joyful, and precious) is nothing apart from Him, and He will help us in our relationships. He will make each of us glad or gleeful (Hebrew word) in our circumstances because He has given (Hebrew words add, apply, appoint, ascribe, assign, coverage, bestow, bring, cast, cause, and charge) us counsel and may I add [good] counsel.

We rejoice (Hebrew word to show influenced emotion) meaning to show happiness in the fullest sense, sing, dance, and really enjoy seeing God's hand as He works out even small areas of challenge. This level of gratitude is a choice and, as the song goes, "Don't wait till the battle is over, shout now! God is at work; rejoice!"

He will show (Hebrew words are: answer, appoint, be aware, advice, consider, discover, can have, instruct, kinsfolk, kinsman, and know [come, to give, have, take] the knowledge needed as He directs our path of life. His presence (Hebrew words are countenance, edge, employ, endure, enquire, face, favor, fear, and forefront) grants us fullness (Hebrew word is satisfied) of joy. At God's right hand are pleasures (Hebrew word is delightfulness) forevermore (eternal) you all!

We must show that God is God to all, so they can come to know Christ and we can be multiplied (Hebrew words enlarge, excel, increase and gather) with great joy. This joy can be maintained (Hebrew words are to bestow, to pass, and to provide) to others as we serve God's kingdom as disciples who are duplicating others to be moved (Hebrew words are carried or be ready) to have a closer relationship with the Lord, because each one enables us to have a life centered with Him.

We bless our Lord for this fullness of joy and that, in Him, His pleasures are evermore. So, Chosen Vessels, allow God to preserve you as you put your trust in Him, because we have a good inheritance waiting for us. Chosen Vessels, set the Lord before you, and place Him at the center of your lives.

What has God revealed to you as you meditate on the scripture?

____

____

____

____

____

____

____

____

____

____

____

____

____

____________________________________ *Journal*

QUESTIONS TO PONDER

A Life Centered on the Lord

1. Have you considered the benefits of godly counsel?
2. What passions await you by centering your thoughts, will, and emotions on God as He bestows His favor on you?
3. Are you willing to keep joy and be ready to posture yourself every day and go the distance no matter what?

Let us pray:

Father we thank you and magnify your holy name. We bless you for placing good counsel in our lives and we continue to gather and be in relationship with you as aim to be ready for our God given assignment for this season of our lives.

What is your prayer today?

____

____

____

____

____

____

____

____

____

____

_______________________________________ *Journal*

Taking Delight in the Revelation of the Lord

Prayer Focus: Psalm 19:1-3, NKJV

The heavens declare the glory of God; And the firmament shows His handiwork. Day unto day utters speech, And night unto night reveals knowledge. *There* is no speech nor language *Where* their voice is not heard.

Prayer Focus Reflection

It is important to take delight in God's Word daily as He fulfills you and you express gratefulness in the Lord. This day let us make God an icon in our lives. It should be a daily desire to walk upright before the Lord, to honor His precepts because He is our master artisan or craftsman…the master artisan that is capable of molding us into the vessels that He has called us to be. The prayer for today is to ask God to connect us tightly to His Word and to other vessels to build a personal relationship with the Lord. As we delight ourselves in God, He will help us to draw near to His spoken and written Word.

Gratitude is what we have because wisdom is our companion in times of trouble and in decision-making times. Psalm 19 serves as a backdrop of the world being formed and reveals how the Lord integrates peace and understanding. Surrendering unto Abba offers a walk in the counsel of God. It gives us a surrounding sound of praise and thanksgiving and a radiant atmosphere filled with peace that surpasses understanding. Daily encounters with the Lord place guidance ahead of us and reveal that there is nothing, absolutely nothing, we cannot face. God's love and protection is greater than anything this world offers.

Jehovah has a divine plan that helps us to lean not to our own understanding but acknowledge Him in all our ways. God promises to be our guiding light and to give us an opening where there seems to be no way out. The destined paths outlined by God serve as the best pathway or gateway to take while traveling this journey of life. We experience great peace when we place our confidence in the Lord Jesus Christ. He is more than able to help us to surrender our ways unto His ways.

Through His divine grace, He helps us to stay connected to Him in our early morning talks, during our afternoon walks, and during our evening strolls. What an impressive God we serve. Let us continue to bless God for being our master craftsman who wrote the plans for this lifestyle. The Lord inhabits our thoughts and our ways, and He enables wisdom to serve as a companion in our day-to-day decision-making. Take time each day to thank God for wisdom being an attribute of your distinguishing character of love, grace, and mercy. After our midnights, new mercy awaits us in the morning because of God's love toward us. God's eternal wisdom pours dewdrops of mercy over our lives. His destiny for us allows us to partake in gaining an understanding as we incline our ear to hear His direction. By walking according to God's precepts, our judgment works best in the counsel of His holiness and righteousness. We are grateful to our Lord God for His love, truth, righteousness, knowledge, and discretion found in His Word. We aim to follow His counsel because it brings us into the conformity of His way. We are so thankful for the wisdom of God.

QUESTIONS TO PONDER

Taking Delight in the Revelation of the Lord

1. What do you hear the Master Artisan saying to you today regarding your purpose?
2. Are you enthusiastic about God's blueprint He made just for you?
3. Are you willing to persevere during pain, trials, and weariness?

Let us pray:

Father help us to take delight in your Word as you reveal your ***purpose*** *and the* ***passion*** *required for us to* ***persevere*** *no matter what. In your name, Jesus, we pray, Amen.*

What is your prayer today?

Journal

PRAYER THEME

Finding Acceptable Words

Prayer Focus: Psalm 19:14, NKJV

Let the words of my mouth and the meditation of my heart Be acceptable in Your sight, O LORD, my strength and my Redeemer.

Prayer Focus Reflection

Wisdom, strength, and grace come from setting up a commitment to read and study God's Word every day. It's so important that our words and thoughts are acceptable in God's sight (Psalm 19:14).

As we meditate on His Word, we are inclining our ears to hear what the Lord wants to say to us. We are to incline our ears to hear where the Lord desires us to walk on His directed path (to keep moving by faith, no matter the mess-ups, the faults, or the imperfections). We are to study His Word and walk in fellowship with Him to equip ourselves to be mighty disciples for His kingdom by keeping His commandments, realizing that old things have passed away, and all things have become new (2 Corinthians 5:17-19). Spend time and allow God to reveal the deeper things of Himself (Ecclesiastes 12:1, 10, 13-14).

- † Realize God is the center of our lives and the great I AM.
- † Engage in daily conversations with Him, and you will experience His grace.

- ✝ Verbalize His praises to everyone you meet.
- ✝ Encourage others to know Jesus as Lord.
- ✝ Always acknowledge Him as the sovereign God.
- ✝ Listen attentively to His commands and believe His Word will heal You.

Chosen Vessels, each day as we read God's Word, as we pray God's Word, we become more mature and less inclined to mingle with what is not pleasing unto God. Our purpose in life is to be a better keeper of our home (spiritual and natural). As we grow daily in Him, let us walk in God's purpose in all that we do. Chosen Vessels, let us take hold of the secret of wholeness, which is to "fear God and keep His commandments." Remember, that our lives are purposed to reflect God's kingdom. Some of us are others first encounter to the Church (body of Christ), so let us remember some wise words, "Words hurt, words heal, how do my words make you feel?"

Let us share the fruit of the Lord's spirit: kindness, gentleness, and meekness. Ecclesiastes 12:14 says,

> *For God will bring every work into judgment, including every secret thing, Whether good or evil.*

QUESTIONS TO PONDER

Finding Acceptable Words

1. What is the purpose of fearing God and keeping His commandments as a keeper of the home (spiritual and natural)?
2. How have your passions helped you to keep God's commandments?
3. Are you willing to persevere and go the distance, no matter what tries to steer you outside of your purpose?

Let us pray:

Lord God Almighty, we Your blood bought Chosen Vessels surrender our hearts, minds, and souls unto You. Reveal to us, Oh Lord the secret things that hinder us and help us to use wise words in our daily conversations so we can please You. We thank You for Your protection and love, Amen.

Journal

PRAYER THEME

The Good Shepherd

Prayer Focus: Psalm 23:1-3, NKJV

The Lord *is* my shepherd; I shall not want. He makes me to lie down in green pastures; He leads me beside the still waters. He restores my soul; He leads me in the path of righteousness For His name's sake.

Prayer Focus Reflection

This twenty-third psalm teaches us that good shepherds are devoted to caring, feeding, and protecting the sheep. As you read the Scripture, remember to take your hands off the situation and trust God. The Lord is our Shepherd, and we shall never want for anything because God offers Himself as our model shepherd. He is our portrait of faithfulness and gives us trustworthy care in every situation or circumstance. He is in control.

Psalm 23 continues to remind us that the Lord promises to care for us because He is our shepherd. As our Shepherd, He will support us. He will give us rest. We can take confidence in knowing that He is more than able to lead us. He will restore us and renew us. He will guide and direct us. He will protect us during storms. He will correct us in a loving manner, and we can take comfort in knowing that He is right there with us in the journey of life. He will give us manna from heaven to feed us spiritually and naturally. He will anoint us with His Word, and He will surround us with His love. Finally, we can take joy in knowing that He is our shelter.

Therefore, Chosen Vessels as you walk this journey of life with the Shepherd right by your side, remember, God is whatever you need Him to be. He has your possessions covered. God will make provision for His children. God will be our peace and give us peace. God is the only one who can pardon us, and He is waiting for us to release our control and allow Him to take full control. As our faithful partner, He is teaching us how to prepare during seasons of lack and fullness. By having our heart filled with praise, we can experience God's rest; and He is more than able to restore.

Therefore, Chosen Vessels, relax, relate, and release your will; because you can let go and let God take the helm!

What has God revealed to you as you meditate on the scripture?

Journal

QUESTIONS TO PONDER

The Good Shepherd

1. What is the purpose of the Lord being your Shepherd?
2. How do you plan to release your passions to help you honor God and allow Him to fill your cup, so that it may overflow?
3. Are you willing to persevere and go the distance, no matter what tries to steer you from relaxing and following the Shepherd?

Let us pray:

Abba Father who art in Heaven, help us connect to a purpose and passion that You have for us as our Shepherd. Teach us, Lord, to persevere no matter what. In your name, Jesus, we pray, Amen.

What is your prayer today?

Journal

PRAYER THEME

Prayer Offers Courage

Prayer Focus: Psalm 27:1, NKJV

The Lord *is* my light and my salvation: Whom shall I fear? The Lord *is* the strength of my life; Of whom shall I be afraid?

Prayer Focus Reflection

Psalm 27 speaks of God being our light and our salvation. Have you ever been in a situation where your way seemed dark? Well, God's Word offers courage, salvation, and light. His Word gives us confidence during sickness, stress at work, and weary relationships. This passage of Scripture allows us to reflect on God's goodness and gives us confidence to continually praise our Lord. Through this passage of Scripture, God helps and instructs us to wait, with God giving us courage. He teaches us to pray with joy, confidence, praise, patience (waiting), and courage.

During pain, we can serve as support for others. We can pray with others and let them know that God gives courage and sanctification to make it through our journey. Daily hold up one another in prayer; text an inspiring word from a Psalm to encourage someone.

Chosen Vessels, it is about having a relationship with Abba Father and bettering our relationships with others. Your encouraging word can ease the stress of the day. We also know that prayer has no bounds; it can travel as far as the east is from the west. So, let us offer support as Chosen Vessel Prayer Warriors.

As you reflect on this Psalm, what words from the Scripture speak to you? Write them down and then pray those words over your situation as Abba will give you courage in the darkest times of Your life.

What has God revealed to you as you meditate on the scripture?

Journal

QUESTIONS TO PONDER

Prayer Offers Courage

1. What is the purpose of prayer for today?
2. Where do your passions lie when you feel weary?
3. Are you willing to persevere during pain, trials, and weariness?

Let us pray:

Abba Father who art in Heaven, we your Chosen Vessels commitment ourselves to walk in our divine purpose as we posture ourselves to pray daily. Help us Lord to fulfill the purposes You have ordained so that we can persevere in our calling. It is in Your name Jesus that is above every name that we pray, Amen.

What is your prayer today?

Journal

A Prayer of Thanks

Prayer Focus: Psalm 30:1-3, NKJV

I will extol You, O Lord, for You have lifted me up, And have not let my foes rejoice over me. O Lord my God, I cried out to You, And You healed me. O Lord, You brought my soul up from the grave; You have kept me alive, that I should not go down to the pit.

Prayer Focus Reflection

Psalm 30 speaks to us of the value of praising God during sickness, illness, and pain. This Psalm teaches us how David understood and appreciated God's ability and power to raise him up from his bed of affliction when he was near death. God heard and answered David's prayers, and He hears and will answer ours as well.

This passage of Scripture focuses on our being able to pray a prayer of thanks:

Abba Father, we are thankful for the opportunity to praise You continually. Your kindness lasts for a lifetime. Your redeeming grace saves us and gives us the ability to never stop praising You. We are thankful for the gladness given unto us. Thank You for regulating our joy, our mind, our happiness through Your favor during the hurt, pain, betrayal, and loneliness. We are so grateful that Your favor lasts a lifetime. We bask in Your presence. Thank You, God, for Your Word gives us hope, faith, and comfort. We can be strong during some difficult days as we know that You are more than able to change our sadness into a morning of gladness. We are thankful for Your being our light amid our weeping in the night and giving us joy in the morning.

Therefore, Chosen Vessels, though this journey may be hard, you are strong. This journey may seem unbearable and even lonely, but you are mighty as a mountain. This journey enables you to grow in God, and we each can take joy in reading, praying, meditating, and believing God's Word. His Word will not return unto us void. By having our heart filled with praise, we can experience God's joy, peace, love, kindness, gladness, and favor.

In addition, remember you are God's temple, blessed, and "girded with gladness." You know that a girdle keeps everything properly placed. Your joy and your relationships serve as a girdle of gladness to someone who needs to connect with the Lord. As your kindness and gladness are given to someone who may not know Christ, help them to experience God's love through your testimony and continue to bless (do a good thing) and praise Him (tell someone of the goodness of Jesus and all that He has done for you). Let others know that they too can experience the depths of Jesus' love, just as you have. Walk in your anointing, walk in your calling, and accept that God has something great in you and in store for you. Continue to praise God and keep Him at the helm of your life!

QUESTIONS TO PONDER

A Prayer of Thanks

1. What is the purpose of prayer for today?
2. Where do your passions lie when you feel weary?
3. Are you willing to persevere during pain, trials, and weariness?

What is your prayer today?

Journal

PRAYER THEME

Prayer Focus: Psalm 34:1-3, NKJV

I will bless the LORD at all times; His praise *shall* continually be in my mouth. My soul shall make its boast in the LORD; The humble shall hear of *it* and be glad. Oh, magnify the LORD with me, And let us exalt His name together.

Prayer Focus Reflection

The purpose of Psalm 34 is to exhort others to share in the blessings of God's protection and His praise. Our spiritual brother, David, purposed and promised to praise the Lord. Throughout Psalm 34, we can experience the acts of God and the attributes of His love toward us.

Chosen Vessels, no matter if we feel afflictions in our relationships, we decree and declare that we will take our eyes off the situation and trust God! We will trust the eyes of the Lord to take us through our situations/ circumstances. As women of God, the Lord will let none of us lack any benefit. As women of God, no matter the season, God's Word says that we "will not lack any good thing!" Marriage is beneficial. Relationships are beneficial. Decree and declare to seek God and stop looking at situations as a dreadful thing because everything we go through is beneficial. The Lord says in Romans 8:28 (NJKV), "And we know that all things work together for good to those who love God, to those who are the called according to His purpose." We are His chosen vessels, suited to handle our situations through communing daily with the Lord.

Our Lord can, shall, and will deliver us from our fears if we trust Him with them. He made everything good. He hears our prayers, and He promises to deliver us. We are to praise Him, trust our Lord, and fear God, not man. The fear of the Lord is honoring Him and respecting His authority over us. He is more than able to restore, repair, and reprove any situation. Chosen Vessels, remember God sees us in whatever condition we are in. He has a steadfast love toward us. No matter where we are, the Lord has His eyes on us. He will direct us to the next level.

When we magnify the Lord, we allow the Lord to expand our thinking and to get engrained in our focus. By choosing to focus on God, then we can guide our focus to the things of the Lord. Even when the enemy seeks to make us think that his ways and thoughts supersede God's, we know better because of God's Word. We know that our God is greater. No matter what it appears to be through our natural eyes, our God is better and bigger than any situation, problem, or circumstance. Let us choose this day to magnify the Lord!

Magnify the Lord, praise Him, and trust Him to deliver us from our fears; take comfort in knowing that the Lord delivers. He is working things out in His timing and in His way. Our life belongs to Him. If we stay focused and remain grounded in praising Him, He will take us to new heights and deeper depths in our relationship with the Him. Remember throughout the journey that God's works and His worth provide the basis for praise. Continue to praise the Lord, for He is worthy of all the praise and honor.

QUESTIONS TO PONDER

Exhorting Others

1. Did you purpose today to speak life and bless others connected to you?
2. Are you a passionate worshipper?
3. As you persevere, what situation causes you to lose focus on the journey and hinders you in magnifying and worshipping the Lord?

Let us pray:

Father we exalt Your Holy name and give You all the praise and the glory. Lord we want to be vessels of honor and we beseech You to direct our path. As we steer off in things that are not like You, we ask You Lord to reposition us to a place that brings You glory, praise, and honor. We thank You Lord for speaking life over us. We bless You and thank you for healing and restoring us. It is in Jesus name we pray and give thanks, Amen.

What is your prayer today?

Journal

PRAYER THEME

Trusting God Grants Righteous Living Benefits

Prayer Focus: Psalm 37:1-3, NKJV

Do not fret because of evildoers, Nor be envious of the workers of iniquity. For they shall soon be cut down like the grass, And wither as the green herb. Trust in the Lord, and do good; Dwell in the land, and feed on His faithfulness.

Prayer Focus Reflection

Psalm 37 tells us that God grants us assurance when we walk in integrity and trust Him. This Psalm teaches us how our spiritual brother, David, understood and appreciated the rewards of righteous living. The Lord uses His written word to speak to us and tells us that it matters to Him that our character reflects righteous living.

The Scripture teaches us to trust God no matter what comes our way. God can lead us when we put our trust in Him. He is needing us to be patient and not become angry because this can lead to sin. Righteous living leads to us being generous people who do not mind giving.

Chosen Vessels, keep giving love and compassion, components of the fruit of the Spirit…fruit that is beneficial to all those you encounter, no matter how they treat you. The Lord tells us when we do our part, He will make certain that each step we take is sure. The Lord will hold our hand, and if we stumble, He will keep us from falling. It is best if we commit to live a righteous lifestyle so we can receive our heart's desire.

God's Word is our daily maintenance, and as we continue to live this life for His glory, we can share our stories to help others to know the King of kings and the Lord of lords. He deserves all the glory and all the praise! Is it not awesome to live this kind of life? So, let us commit to not be annoyed or controlling, but instead choose to be surrendered vessels whose purpose is to live a life of integrity and peace. God is our shelter, a secure refuge, in times of trouble. By trusting God, He will help us to be patient. He will deliver us from our fears. He will give us wisdom.

Remember, Chosen Vessels, the Lord is our shelter, cover, protector, keeper, and way maker, so no worries. We decree and declare to walk in His peace because we can **trust God** to keep us safe. He will lead us with His wisdom, and He will grant us peace. We leave the pain of the past and press toward the future grounded in God's will and plan for our lives. We thank God for connecting us to a local church body. We thank Him for connecting us to another sister for our journey. We thank God for being our personal Savior and know that as we seek first the kingdom of God that all things will be added unto us. If we trust God with all our heart, and lean not to our own understanding, He promises to direct our path. Chosen Vessels, great benefits come from righteous living. Choose this day to be stronger, wiser, and better. Continue to praise and bless His holy name.

QUESTIONS TO PONDER

Trusting God Grants Righteous Living Benefits

1. Did you purpose today to speak life and bless others connected to you?
2. Are you a passionate worshipper?
3. As you persevere, what situation causes you to lose focus on the journey and hinders you in magnifying and worshipping the Lord?

Let us pray:

King of kings and Lord of lords, we come to You with our hands raised and with a praise on our lips. We ask You, Lord, to help us live a righteous life and connect to Your ways and Your thoughts as outlined in Your Word. Help us become more passionate people who persevere no matter what. In Your name, Jesus, we pray, Amen.

What is your prayer today?

____

____

____

____

____

____

____

____

____

_________________________________ *Journal*

PRAYER THEME

Seeing Him

Prayer Focus: Psalm 41:1-3, NKJV

Blessed *is* he who considers the poor; The Lord will deliver him in time of trouble. The Lord will preserve him and keep him alive, *And* he will be blessed on the earth; You will not deliver him to the will of his enemies. The Lord will strengthen him on his bed of illness; You will sustain him on his sickbed.

Prayer Focus Reflection

The purpose of Psalm 41 is for us to know He will show mercy to the weak and protect us from our enemies. God will not allow the enemy to overtake us. Abba grants us sustaining power, and He will keep us when we are ill (spiritually, emotionally, and physically).

Therefore, Chosen Vessels, let us stand our ground, declare today our commitment to see Him in all that we do. Stand firm and believe that the Lord will deliver and supply healing. The Lord promises us triumph over any situation that may try to overtake our lives. We need only to cry out to our Lord for a natural and a spiritual healing. We need to ask for a spiritual restoration in any relationship that needs a healing and be thankful to God for His healing power.

As we declare God's Word back to Him, we speak deliverance over our families. We decree and declare unity and the power of one accord during our relationships. We know that the Lord is with us. He is in the midst and will draw us closer to Him. We decree and declare to esteem others, because everything is about us helping others. We declare that on this journey of life, we will consider the poor in spirit, the poor in finances, and we will share our story. We will let others know that the Lord is more than able to deliver us in our times of trouble. We understand that charity begins at home, and we must begin by loving and forgiving ourselves first.

We decree and declare that we will hold ourselves in a posture of repentance. We ask the Lord to forgive us of our sins of not showing mercy and grace or not managing the resources that He has given us. We ask the Lord to show us ourselves and create in us a clean and contrite spirit that understands the value in being honest with God and ourselves. We commit to walk in a spirit of forgiveness and integrity because we are His chosen vessels. Once we are in a posture of repentance, then we can walk in our healing, be it physical, emotional, or spiritual. We stand in agreement that the Lord will restore and that we will assume a posture of forgiveness, morning, noon, and night. Maintaining such a posture will allow us to begin to see God's love triumph, and we will see Him change our situations.

The Lord is merciful because we all have sinned and fallen short of God's glory, but He gave us a promise that His mercies will last forever and ever. God's mercy stands for a double blessing. The Lord is pleased with us, and our reward stems from our relationship with Him. We commit to change our tone and commit our hearts and our minds to God. Our God will strengthen, and He is the only one who can sustain us. He is the vine of our life. Walk in your emotional, physical, and spiritual healing. Remember this: God cares for us, and we commit to praise Him, see Him, and remain faithful to Him. Continue to praise the Lord.

QUESTIONS TO PONDER

Seeing Him

1. Have you purposed today to "see Him" in every situation?
2. Are you enthusiastic about sharing your testimony with others?
3. Are you willing to persevere and go the distance no matter what?

Let us pray:

Our Creator, Your Majesty, our Savior and Lord, we come to You and kneel before You to request that You, dear Lord, help us to see You. Help us connect to a purpose and passion that You have for us. Teach us, Lord, to persevere no matter what. In Your name, Jesus, we pray, Amen.

What is your prayer today?

Journal

A Royal Wedding for God's Daughters of Righteousness

Prayer Focus: Psalm 45:1-3, NKJV

My heart is overflowing with a good theme; I recite my composition concerning the King; My tongue *is* the pen of a ready writer. You are fairer than the sons of men; Grace is poured upon Your lips: Therefore, God has blessed you forever. Gird Your sword upon *Your* thigh, O Mighty One, With Your glory and Your majesty.

Prayer Focus Reflection

Psalm 45 teaches us that God desires preparation before we meet Him. In this Psalm, we learn how much the groom loves His bride, and He finds her beautiful. The Lord uses His written Word to speak to us and tells us to worship the King; we are declaring our love to Him. We have promised to love the Lord with all our heart, all our mind, and all our soul (Deuteronomy 6:5). Our praise of the King should reflect a posture of a ready writer. As we share the goodness of the Lord with others, we can help to win others to the kingdom.

God's Word clothes us with His righteousness. What does this mean? It means that He has given us a gift of goodness because of our belief in Him as our Messiah. Clothing ourselves with humility or meekness gives us the ability to rise and ride victoriously with God because He gives us His strength. We know that God can work things out for our good. As God's prayer warriors, we need to prepare and equip ourselves so that we can be ready for battle, knowing He protects.

Chosen Vessels, just as the bride adorns herself for her groom, so does God adorn us in preparation for His coming. In addition, He prepares us for war on the battlefield, and we must be ready for His return. Marriage unites the family, which the enemy seeks to destroy, but the Lord has given us a weapon of prayer to fight the enemy and put him under our feet. God knows and provides us with our spiritual weapons of warfare. Our Lord hates wickedness, and He grants us an opportunity to repent so we can be His daughters of righteousness. Psalm 45 encourages women that the King of kings loves them, and He is speaking to their self-esteem. He declares in Psalm 45:11 that the,

> "Lord is enthralled by His bride's beauty and that His love for her is above all loves. His love is standing at the throne awaiting His bride to meet Him." Oh, when we see Him and look upon His face!

Queen Esther serves as a biblical role model. Her testimony offers encouragement to stay with God as His bride. Queen Esther's story reminds us that we too should be willing to perish for our King's glory. As she was willing to perish for her commitment to save her people, she stood, willing to die for truth and justice.

I love this statement, "Oh, to be the Bride of Christ, scented with spices, and adorned with oil, [knowing] that the Lord is so glad to see us." God is willing to incline His ear to our every need, and He loves us so much that He has a place prepared just for us. My heart beats for that day!

You know, Chosen Vessels, God prepared a place for us, and He desires us to surrender, hold fast, and yield to Him through total dependence. As you seek God, listen to His instruction on the benefits of being humble Chosen Vessels. God's Word is our daily maintenance. As we clothe ourselves in humility and study God's Word, we can better understand being humble in spirit because of His redemptive love toward us.

Daughters of righteousness, you have an inward beauty, and you are committed to becoming His bride and sharing your joy with others, so they too can become a son and daughter of the Most High God. Remember, Chosen Vessels, the Lord is captivated with our beauty. Give ear to our Lord and remember to love Him with all your heart, soul, and might. Let us commit to instruct our children about the Lord and talk to God throughout the day, night, and early waking morning. Finally, read and adhere to Matthew 22:37-40 (NKJV). This passage of Scripture tells us of the first and greatest commandment, which is to love the Lord God and to love our neighbor as ourselves.

Therefore, Chosen Vessels, function as a ready writer in an audience of our God. He is the only one that matters because He sees and hears all. We are not perfect; only God is, but He grants us the wisdom to become mature and strive to be His faithful servants. Allow God's fruit of the Spirit to serve as your guide, and let your praises and lifestyle reflect His thoughts.

QUESTIONS TO PONDER

A Royal Wedding from God's Daughters of Righteousness

1. Have you purposed today to be a ready writer in every situation?
2. Are you passionate about sharing your testimony with others?
3. Are you willing to persevere and go the distance no matter what?

What is your prayer today?

____

____

____

____

____

____

____

____

____

____

____

____

____

____

_____________________________________ *Journal*

PRAYER THEME

God, Our Guide for Every Situation

Prayer Focus: Psalm 48:1-3, NKJV

Great *is* the Lord, and greatly to be praised *In* the city of our God, In His holy mountain. Beautiful in elevation, The joy of the whole earth, *Is* Mount Zion *on* the sides of the north, The city of the great King. God *is* in her palaces; He is known as her refuge.

Prayer Focus Reflection

Psalms 48 lets us know that we are His righteous people who should praise God because He is praiseworthy. No matter our situation, the Lord is our guide as well as our great King. Our King is a righteous God who can and will answer our prayers. He is our bulwark, or one could say our wall of hope. Abba is a solid, wall-like structure in our lives, which stands for our fortified wall of hope, praise, and adoration.

During this season, we are to share God's Word and help our families, friends, and foes know God. We are not to be afraid to worship Him in spirit and in truth. As we share God's Word and tell others of His goodness, we help others to know Him and the power of His Word.

Therefore, Chosen Vessels, if you feel helpless and hopeless, know that the Lord is our refuge and strength. He is our strong tower. He is there for us horizontally and vertically. He is our God who will help us develop our relationships.

As we ponder on Psalm 48, we glean that the Scripture signifies God is our fortress. God set before us a mirror that represents God's character that can be seen through His many attributes. The Lord has invested in each of us, and we are to take on His character and tell others of His character. God's character traits reflect His integrity, faithfulness, and steadfast love (which never ceases) and His patience toward us. God's mercies are new every morning (Psalm 30 and Lamentations 3:22-23, NKJV). Thank you, Jehovah-Jireh, Jehovah Shalom.

God's love daily fortifies us. To fortify is to be equipped with endurance. He has given us an opportunity to "take note of the fortified walls, and tour all the citadels, that you may describe them to future generations," Psalm 48:13 (NKJV). We can tell our sons, our daughters, our siblings, our parents, and those who do not know the Lord that we have power to endure our situations. Share the Gospel with all who will hear and help others to take strength in their circumstances. Praying God's Word allows us to add mental or moral strength, to encourage others and fortify one another to pray without ceasing. So, pray a hedge of fortified walls around your family and your friends.

Look upward horizontally, believe God vertically, and allow others to go to the Cross and seek God's refuge. He is our guide. As our guide, He is our hiding place and our protection during the storms. Ask God to place a hedge of fortified walls around you for every situation.

QUESTIONS TO PONDER

God, Our Guide for Every Situation

1. Have you purposed in your heart to submit to God in every situation of your life?

2. Will you align God's purpose to fill your passions with God's strength?

3. Are you willing to persevere and allow God to be your guide and go the distance no matter what?

What is your prayer today?

Journal

PRAYER THEME

Experience Peace When God is in Control

Prayer Focus: Psalm 52:1-3, NKJV

Why do you boast in evil, O mighty man? The goodness of God *endures* continually. Your tongue devises destruction, Like a sharp razor, working deceitfully. You love evil more than good, Lying rather than speaking righteousness. *Selah*

Prayer Focus Reflection

Today's prayer focus is on God destroying the wicked as He destroyed Doeg the Edomite. Doeg betrayed David and his men to King Saul when he told King Saul that David had gone to the house of Ahimelech. As you know, God's Word speaks loud and clear of a daily lesson for righteous living. He allows His Word to be a beckon of light to our life's path. His Word calms fears, settles emotions, and helps us to walk by the Spirit. Praise and thank God for His written Word and spoken Word, as it is a beam of light during dark periods of life.

History tells us that during this period of Psalm 52 that David had been anointed king of Israel, but Saul did not want to relinquish his throne. During this time, God protected David using Saul's own son, Jonathan. Is that not like the Lord? The enemy thinks he has us, and then the Lord allows us to have a way of escape. Jonathan, who loved David, gave his friend a word that enabled David to flee to a safe place, the house of Ahimelech. Then during this Psalm, David ran to a dark cave to seek protection. Just as God supplied David protection, He will do the same for us.

From David's experience, he learned in Psalm 52:1 that the "goodness of God endures (withstands) continually." He learned in Psalm 52:7 that God would be his strength. He learned in Psalm 52:8 that he considered himself "like a green olive tree in the house of God." A green olive tree signified that David could live in peace, prosperity, and wealth because he was a child of God. A child of God experiences benefits when he or she makes God his strength (power, force, might, and courage). In this walk, we each should want to "be like a tree planted by the rivers of water, That brings forth his fruit in its season" Psalm 1:3 (NKJV).

Chosen Vessels, our protection is tied to our faith, and faith fuels perseverance. God is our protection, and His power protects us. David held on to his faith and did not give up. Let God remove the strongholds within your life and place your absolute trust in the living God. Know that He fulfills His promises. Just as God was in control of David's life and He protected him, He will protect us.

God speaks daily to us as Chosen Vessels, and you should allow His Word to speak to you. Call upon Him. Realize that you can find comfort in God for every waking moment. Call upon the many names of God for every situation that you need. If you wake up in the middle of the night and find yourself unable to go back to sleep, call upon the name of Jesus and ask the Prince of Peace to rock you back to sleep. Take God's Word and speak it over your life. It is written in Matthew 8:7 (NKJV) that "Jesus said to him, 'I will come and heal him.'"

God's Word is a confirming Word, and He can put a hedge of protection around each of us through His power, wisdom, and might to heal us.

God's Word is flourishing, and it helps us to thrive when we are pressed down and shaken by troubling situations. His Word can lift us up when we are tempted to consider crazy things due to a lack of trusting God to turn things around. Many times, some of us have lacked faith and trust in Him for making things right. However, once we surrender and give God our all by making Him first, we can flourish like the olive tree in the house of God.

Being like the sheltered olive tree surrounded by God's protection should be our goal. We must make daily resolutions to allow God to be our strength. Then, as we walk in God's power, we can begin to walk in God's anointing due to our being strengthened by the Holy One. Life circumstances can contaminate our temples and our homes, but our focus must remain on God's ability to strengthen us to make it. Abba will take care of the wicked who try to dismantle us. Our Lord will pluck the wicked out of their dwelling place, and He will uproot them. God's Word reminds us to trust in the mercy of God forever, because we are firmly planted and rooted in God's Word.

Chosen Vessels, let us commit to ask God to renew our faith. Let us reaffirm that God is in control. Let us daily reflect on God's reign over our lives. Allow God to plant His Word in our hearts so we can experience His overflow of power, presence, and protection. Reflect on Psalm 52:9a (NKJV) and "praise [our God] forever, Because [He has] done it." Done what? He has delivered us from a bad habit or attitude, inappropriate thoughts, or a deceitful tongue.

Chosen Vessels, our Lord is good. His name is above every name, and we can hold on to His Word because surely [His] goodness and mercy shall follow [us] all the days of [our] life; and [we] will dwell in the house of the Lord forever (Psalm 23:6, NKJV). Amen.

QUESTIONS TO PONDER

Experience Peace When God is in Control

1. Have you purposed today to experience God's goodness in every situation of your life?
2. Are you passionate about sharing your testimony with others?
3. Are you willing to persevere and go the distance no matter what?

What is your prayer today?

Journal

PRAYER THEME

Trusting God

Prayer Focus: Psalm 55:1-3, NKJV

Give ear to my prayer, O God, And do not hide Yourself from my supplication. Attend to me, and hear me; I am restless in my complaint, and moan noisily, Because of the voice of the enemy, Because of the oppression of the wicked; For they bring down trouble upon me, And in wrath they hate me.

Prayer Focus Reflection

Psalm 55 speaks of the common human frailties of betrayal and deception. Sometimes, it is harder for us to deal with betrayal by someone we value. However, our spiritual brother, David, gives us an example of how to make our requests known unto God. Yes, God knows everything about us, and He always grants us an opportunity to converse with Him. David prayed three times a day, and scriptures tell us that some prophets prayed up to seven times a day. His format of prayer may serve as an outline to daily feed our souls by praying unto our God. David prayed for God's help in every situation as he prayed in the morning, at noon, and at night.

Fear of the enemy may have been David's frailty at heart. However, by facing those fears or shortcomings head on, David learned how important it was for him to pray and pour out his heart to God. As David saw, we, too, will see that the Lord can sustain us because He is our covering. We just need to trust God because He will be our stream in the desert. As we cast our burdens on the Lord, He gives us the ability to stand and trust Him. He hears us and teaches us how to be still and see His salvation. God's love will destroy our fears, and He will encourage us through His Word. Even when our lives feel upside down, our individual walk will make us better in our personal relationship with our Father, our Lord, our Savior and Redeemer. God's Word helps us to purge what needs purging. He conditions our soul.

Therefore, if we trust God and cast our burdens on Him, He will sustain and comfort us. We may be scared, shaking and wondering what is going to happen next, but we have a promise during our battles. Battles may come from those closest to us or those at a distance. The Lord will help us regardless of the situation in which we find ourselves. In Psalm 55:16-17 (NKJV), we too can talk to God as David did and say…

> But, I will call to [You] God for help. And…Lord [You have promised]…to save me. [No matter, how I feel in the] morning, noon, and night [and when I am feeling] troubled and upset. [You oh Lord] will listen to me.

As we see in this passage of Scripture, Psalm 55:16-17 (NKJV), David prayed to the Lord. He spoke to Him from his heart, from his pain, and from his inner terror or fears. The Lord hears us. No matter what state we are in, He can turn the upside-down or right side up. Let us practice similar principles to what David did and talk to God in the morning, at noon, and at night.

For seven minutes today, give God your waking thoughts so He can help you balance your day. During this quiet time or moment of stillness or silence, journal your thoughts. As God speaks, write down what you hear, then select three words that speak to you. Whisper a prayer, stop, and listen for the call and response. God will respond, so incline your ear to hear; listen and allow your mind to rest on His thoughts.

QUESTIONS TO PONDER

Trusting God

1. Have you purposed in your heart today to give God your waking, waiting, and whispered thoughts?
2. Will you allow the passionate prayer warrior to awaken inside of you?
3. Are you willing to persevere, even if awakened by a middle-of-the-night wakeup call from God Himself?

What is your prayer today?

Journal

PRAYER THEME

Prayer Focus: Psalm 59:1-3, NKJV

Deliver me from my enemies, O my God; Defend me from those who rise up against me. Deliver me from the workers of iniquity, And save me from bloodthirsty men. For look, they lie in wait for my life; The mighty gather against me, Not *for* my transgression nor *for* my sin, O LORD.

Prayer Focus Reflection

Today's prayer focus is on God's promise of assured judgment of the wicked. David desired God to deliver him from his enemies, so he called unto the Lord. David's enemies had set out to kill him, but David had an offensive weapon—the weapon of prayer. Chosen Vessels, we are called to watch and pray each day. Some of you may wonder why you are awakening at 3:00 a.m. or 5:00 a.m. This is the fourth watch of prayer of the night. We are called to be God's watchmen, and our prayers can combat the enemy. God promised us that we will overcome, and today's word enables you to feast on God's promise to you.

The Lord gives us authority to reach out to Him in Jeremiah 33:3 (NKJV). He tells us to:

> "Call unto [Him] and [He] will answer [us] and show [us] great and mighty things that [we] do not know."

God's Word protects us, and His Word tells us His mercy shall come to meet us. Wherever we are, God will meet us and bring deliverance to us, but we must seek Him first! When we seek God first, we can expect our healing, deliverance, protection, and a breakthrough. We can pray God's Word in a comparable manner.

Let us pray:

Lord, we pray that You will protect us, and we speak life over the bloodthirsty who seek to destroy us. We pray Your defense for the iniquities of injustice and ask You, Lord, to deliver us from prejudice and fear. Lord, we adore You and thank You for forgiving us and meeting our need. Thank You for freedom and healing. We pray a hedge of protection around our family, and we hedge our family with Your Word.

We ask you to embrace our family as we yield to Your power and grace as our protector. You, oh God, are our Lamb of God, and we adore You, for You mean all the world to us. We pray strength for our families, and we ask that You destroy everything that seeks to counter Your perfect will. We pray that You, oh, Lord, will help our family to come to know You and commit themselves to Your will and Your way. We pray, Lord, that You deliver our families and, as our defender, we stand on Your Word and ask You, dear Lord, to help us not to be afraid of the barking dogs that seek to devour us. We pray, Lord, that You will teach us to wait on You and, by doing so, gain renewed strength. Help us to cease from leaning on our own understanding, but to acknowledge You in all our ways. We praise

You, dear Lord, and wait on You, dear Lord, as our defender. We know You will deliver us from our struggle.

Therefore, we decree and declare that we surrender ourselves unto the Lord, and we remember that we are His watchful Chosen Vessels who are called to wait on the wall, stand in the gap, and use our offensive weapon of prayer. Amen.

Chosen Vessels, remember time is essential. When the Lord calls you during your appointed watch, answer the call, go in prayer on behalf of others for whom God directs you to pray, and begin to call unto our Lord. You can pray one word or several words. Our God hears us, and we can thank Him for being a prayer answering God. Sing a Psalm unto God, and let it become a song of praise to whatever you have encountered or will encounter because the Lord is our refuge, defense, strength, and deliver from the bloodthirsty enemy!

At whatever time God awakens you and speaks to you, cover yourself and your family, ministry, work, property, and nation with the blood of Jesus. Pray a Psalm aloud and proclaim that your family and the nation will be a disciple to God. We decree and declare healing and restoration to God's kingdom by His blood and the power that His Word testifies to them that seek a more intimate relationship with the Lord. We decree and declare God's Word, for it is His kingdom, His power, His glory, and His will which shall be done forever and ever, Amen!

QUESTIONS TO PONDER

Prayers for Protection

1. Have you considered to purpose in your heart to cast your hopes, dreams, and aspirations in the hands of Abba Father?
2. Will you allow your passionate prayer warrior to awaken inside of you?
3. Are you willing to persevere, even if awakened by a middle-of-the-night wakeup call from God Himself?

What is your prayer today?

Journal

Strengthening Faith and Hope

Prayer Focus: Psalm 62:1-3, NKJV

Truly my soul silently *waits* for God; From Him *comes* my salvation. He only *is* my rock and my salvation; He *is* my defense; I shall not be greatly moved. How long will you attack a man? You shall be slain, all of you, Like a leaning wall and a tottering fence.

Prayer Focus Reflection

During my study time, I ran across this quote: "Meditation and prayer are blessed means of strengthening faith and hope." It reminded me that we each have the strength that we need because of our faith in God and the knowledge that He is our hope. Hope requires trusting God, so when we are in doubt, remember that the Lord will supply our every need and protect us during our storms of life. What each of us must do is place our wishes, dreams, hopes, aspirations, and expectations in God. Trust God to supply your need and strengthen you.

We all need a daily word. The Lord speaks through His Chosen Vessels. Therefore, incline your ear to hear; lay your wants, dreams, hopes, aspirations, and expectations before the Lord and then patiently wait on Him. Submit your will to His will and pour out your heart before Him.

God is our refuge, and He will give us the shelter we need. We are to trust God, not man. Let us place our confidence in God and trust Him with every situation, great or small. Remember what the Lord said in Psalm 62:7-8:

> In God is my salvation and my glory; The rock of my strength, And my refuge, is in God. Trust in Him at all times, you people; Pour out your heart before Him; God is a refuge for us.

God balances our lives with His Word. Hold on to your word and take heed to what He speaks to you during your moment of stillness or time of reflection. Take five or ten minutes, meditate on His Word, and allow His Word to draw you closer unto Him. Trust God and wait on Him for all things always. Always place your expectations in God, not man. Spend some moments of silence in His presence.

Know that God is always your strength in all things. Our God, our Lord, is our solid rock that is higher than we can ever be or become. Take time and allow the Lord to speak to you; incline your ear to hear. Do not allow man to be a stronghold in your life. In addition, close your day by allowing God to minister to you.

QUESTIONS TO PONDER

Strengthening Faith and Hope

1. Have you purposed in your heart today to wait on the Lord who is your strength?
2. Will you all the passionate prayer warrior inside of you to awaken?
3. Are you willing to persevere, even if awakened by a middle-of-the-night wakeup call from God Himself?

What is your prayer today?

Journal

PRAYER THEME

Praising and Worshiping the Lord

Prayer Focus: Psalm 66:1-3, NKJV

Make a joyful shout to God, all the earth! Sing out the honor of His name; Make His praise glorious. Say to God, "How awesome are Your works! Through the greatness of Your power Your enemies shall submit themselves to You."

Prayer Focus Reflection

Today's prayer focus is on our praising and worshiping God. We are to offer God sacrifices of praise. As you may recall from an earlier entry, we are called to watch and pray each day. As God's called, anointed, and appointed watchmen (watchwomen), this call enables our prayers to combat the enemy. Satan's imps will tremble at God's mighty power and everyone will bow down to Him.

The focused words for today are *praise* and *worship*. In God, we have life and we have it more abundantly, which means a place of plenty. Psalm 66:12 says, "…We went through fire and through water; yet You have brought us out to a place of abundance." Finally, it says in Psalm 66:16-17:

> "Come and hear, all you who fear God, and I will tell what he has done for my soul. I cried to him with my mouth, and high praise was on my tongue" (meaning He was exalted with my tongue).

Today, let us pray prayers of worship and adoration unto Him:
Lord, we thank You for Your steadfast love that never ceases. We worship You, Lord, in spirit and in truth. We honor You with divine confidence in Your Spirit and Truth. We pray, Lord, that You will refine us and that, through our refinement, You will fulfill Your purpose in our life. Each test that we go through, we know this fire will fulfill us and make us wealthy with Your anointing and grace. Lord, the vow that each of us has taken, we are promising to fulfill Your deeds and speak boldly, share love and encouragement with others, and delight in Your way through songs of praise and worship. Father, we respectfully fear You, Lord, and we ask You to help us not forget to reference You in every situation of our lives. Lord, we thank You for Your mercy and that You did not turn away from us. We thank You for granting us new mercies every morning. Lord, we are grateful that You take us through our storms in life. We thank You that You bring us through the storms of life and carry us over the storm to the other side. Dear King, we thank You for listening to every concern and every groan. Father, we worship, honor, praise and adore You. Lord, we thank You for preserving and protecting us. Help us to remain steadfast and keep our foot from slipping because You, dear Lord, heard our prayer this day. We corporately thank You for everything.

Therefore, we decree and declare as yielded vessels that we surrender to the Almighty God. We aim to stand at the gate, stand at our post, and bless You, God, for "...listening; You, dear Lord, have attended to the voice of [our] prayers…and we bless You, O God, because You have not rejected [our prayers] or removed Your steadfast love from [us] (Based on Psalm 66:19-20).

Chosen Vessels, remember time is essential; when the Lord calls you during your appointed watch, answer the call, enter the throne room promptly to pray on behalf others. Our God hears us, and we can sing and shout praises unto God for attending to our prayers. Bombard heaven and embrace His love; allow the words of Psalm 66:16-20 to become your song of praise to whatever you have encountered or will meet this day.

At whatever time God awakens and speaks to you, cover yourself and your family, ministry, work, property, and nation with the blood of Jesus, and daily pray a Psalm aloud and proclaim that your family and nation will become His disciples. We decree and declare healing and restoration to God's kingdom by His blood and the power that His Word testifies to them that seek a more intimate relationship with the Lord. We decree and declare God's Word for it is His kingdom, power, glory, and that will be done forever and ever, amen!

QUESTIONS TO PONDER

Praising and Worshiping the Lord

1. Have you purposed in your heart today to praise God continually?
2. Will you allow your passionate prayer warrior to awaken inside of you?
3. Are you willing to persevere, even if awakened by a middle-of-the-night wakeup call from God Himself?

What is your prayer today?

Journal

PRAYER THEME

Treading Deep Waters

Prayer Focus: Psalm 69:1-3, NKJV

Save me, O God! For the waters have come up to *my* neck. I sink in deep mire, Where *there* is no standing; I have come into deep waters, Where the floods overflow me. I am weary with my crying; My throat is dry; My eyes fail while I wait for my God.

Prayer Focus Reflection

Psalm 69 lets us know that we will get tired, frustrated, and a little flabbergasted! However, through those emotions, God knows, and God hears. It may seem like God is not there and that He is not moving fast enough because, as Psalm 69:1-3 says, David felt as if he was drowning in the deep waters of life. No matter how deep the waters are the Lord can help us to tread through them. Water represents the Holy Spirit, and the Holy Spirt can protect us. He is our salvation and will keep us during our despair and grant us persistence and hope because He is the great I AM. The I AM is our provider, our hope, and our shield.

Chosen Vessels, you are an overcomer. As an overcomer, you are to humble yourself. Then, at the opportune time, the Lord will rescue you from your situation that appears to be muddy, deep waters. How do I know? God's Word says in Psalm 69:16 (NKJV) that…

> The Lord's lovingkindness *is* good [sweet and comforting] and our …Lord has tender mercy and [a steadfast love toward us].

Chosen Vessels, praise the name of God with a song and magnify Him with thanksgiving and live for God's purpose because He hears our cries. Keep the faith, remember God has a purpose for you, and walk in your purpose.

What has God revealed to you as you meditate on the scripture?

Journal

QUESTIONS TO PONDER

Treading Deep Waters

1. Have you considered if your purpose has staggered because you are tired and feel overtaken while treading deep waters?
2. Do you think that your passions seem unbalanced because of your emotions?
3. Are you willing to persevere in the deep waters of life?

What is your prayer today?

Journal

PRAYER THEME

God Is Good: To Suffer is to Reign with Him

Prayer Focus: Psalm 73:1-3, NKJV

Truly God *is* good to Israel, To such as are pure in heart. But as for me, my feet had almost stumbled; My steps had nearly slipped. For I *was* envious of the boastful, When I saw the prosperity of the wicked.

Prayer Focus Reflection

Today's prayer focus is on our learning that God is good and that there are prospects of good and of evil. What do we mean when we say prospects? *Merriam Webster Dictionary* defines *prospects* as *the possibility that something will happen in the future or an opportunity for something to happen.* Chosen Vessels, today's prayer focus gives us vision with a purpose. I understand with a greater revelation that this journey is about us being holy.

Psalm 73 offers instruction and deals with not just suffering but a definition of God's goodness. In life, trouble and struggles will come, as depicted in Psalms 73:2-28. This Psalm explains that as God's people, we will have doubts; but God orders our steps, and He can take us through the valley. He has the power and grace to bring us to the mountaintop as we continue to show our renewed faith, praise Him, and give devotion to our good God. Do you remember the phrase in Scripture that says, "no cross, no crown"? Read more in James 1:12 (NKJV) and Revelation 2:10 (NKJV). The joy comes because we know that our God is powerful, great, and the one who rewards our diligently seeking Him. In the midst of suffering, let us believe God's Word, which says in Psalm 73:24,

> You will guide me with Your counsel. And afterward receive me *to* glory.

God's guidance will help us during times we feel as if we are losing a grip on circumstances and becoming emotionally unstable. Sometimes our emotions can make us feel envious. Yes, I said it: sometimes, I get envious in thinking that the enemy is advancing, but that is when I really see me. You know speaking the truth makes you free. This liberation allowed me to reflect on my need for Jesus to cover and guide me with His counsel. When we speak truth over our situations, Abba will restore us.

Let us pray for times when we lose our grip:

Lord, we need You to help us persevere in hope. We ask that You keep us during restoration and allow us to grow closer to You, so we can go deeper. We want to be in and accept Your perfect will. Lord, as we enter Your sanctuary and begin to daily commune with You, this enables us to get closer to You. We thank You for the one-on-one fellowship in Your presence, and that we can take rest in Your counsel. Thank You, Lord for reminding us that the wicked have their own destination (Psalm 73:17).

Jehovah God, thank You for Your tender mercies and loving kindness, which are our door posts to victory during pain. Father, we bless You that You promise to guide us as You receive us in Your glory. Thank You for giving us an opportunity to live according to Your will and to know that, during our pain, we see that life is temporary, but Your love is steadfast and everlasting. Lord God help us not to be foolish but to continually seek You and take refuge in Your way.

Father allow us to walk in Your strength and fulfill our purpose in Your hope, joy, and peace because we know Your Word is faithful. Lord, Jesus, we thank You that You enable us to draw near unto You during our troubles. We thank You for Your strength to carry us and Your love to forgive us and Your wisdom that orders our steps and prepares our way (Psalm 73:28). Jesus, we say nevertheless You have promised to guide us and give us counsel. After all the pain, disappointment, and even misunderstandings, we know You continually walk with us and cover us with Your power (Psalms 73:23). Lord, we want only You. Father, You are everything to us. You are our overall, and we will forever praise Your holy name in Your holy place (Psalm 73:24, 26). Thank You, Lord, for guidance and strength during abandonment and loneliness. You, dear Lord, have granted us Your strength, favor, and grace during this difficult season. Thank You, Lord, for Your joy, salvation, and glorious destiny that has been pre-planned by Your Word and purposed for our lives. Lord, thank You for making our lives healthy and whole by reading, studying, and praying Your Word.

Father, we close this prayer with a declaration of Your Word over our lives. We decree and declare that Your goodness, mercy, and grace shall always be our passageway. We decree and declare that this journey will be for our good because Your Word says, "in all things we are to give thanks...because all things work together for our good."

Finally, we stand on Psalm 73:28 (NKJV)...

> *[Nevertheless], it is good (desirable, pleasant, favorable, and right) for [us] to draw near to God; [We] have put [our] trust in the Lord God, That [we] may declare (confidently proclaim) all Your works.*

Lord, help us to incline our ears to hear You and surrender unto Your love. Amen.

QUESTIONS TO PONDER

God is Good: To Suffer is to Reign with Him

1. Have you considered if your purpose aligns with the goodness of God?
2. Do you think that your passions seem unbalanced because of your lack of trust?
3. Are you willing to persevere in the deep waters in this journey of life?

What is your prayer today?

Journal

God's Timing

Prayer Focus: Psalm 75:1-3, NKJV

We give thanks to You, O God, we give thanks! For Your wondrous works declare *that* Your name is near. When I choose the proper time, I will judge uprightly. The earth and all its inhabitants are dissolved; I set up its pillars firmly.

Prayer Focus Reflection

This passage of Scripture in Psalms serves as pillars of hope. It offers us a personal roadmap for our lives and gives us daily words to pray and sing to express our emotions.

Let us give thanks to our God for His wondrous works and declare that His name is near as we see in Psalm 75:1. In Psalm 75, we see that God does not operate on our timeline. He chooses the proper time for judgment and deliverance. In Psalm 75, Sennacherib was King of Assyria (part of Iraq). He attacked Judah, the fourth son of Jacob and Leah. During David's time, Assyria was a strong country found to the north and east of Judah. Sennacherib attacked Judah, but he did not win the war; in fact, he lost many of his soldiers during this battle.

The Lord protected Jerusalem. Jerusalem means Salem, which means "peace" or "no fighting." In addition, Jerusalem means Zion, which is the name of the hill where the Israelites built their temple, the place where they met to praise God. When you are in a battle, praise God and know that the Lord will bring peace. Our God will shield our mind and give us courage.

Psalm 75 speaks about how God dealt with those who came into God's den; He devoured the enemy. In verses 1 and 2, God lets us know that He is our God who can break the enemy. No matter what fiery weapons the enemy tries to shoot, the Lord is our shield, the Lord is our sword, and the enemy's weapons cannot compare. Our God spoke of His dwelling place, His place of refuge, His place of strength. Psalm 46, 47, 48, and 75 teach us more about that. Remember that the Lord will defeat any enemy that tries to beset our lives. Let us respond in a godly manner because God is our keeper. We are not to take God lightly because His Word is worth keeping. Let us stop taking things so personally and understand that a godly response works best. Chosen Vessels, allow God's Word and lifestyle to teach you self-control, because everything that God has for us brings Him glory.

Allow this passage of Scripture to speak to you. Use God's Word as written in this Psalm to lead you on this journey of life. The Lord has set a time for your deliverance. His Word does not return void, and He keeps telling us that He is in control and is our refuge and strength. Our God is awesome, and we are to worship Him and Him alone. God will tell us what to do and when to do it.

Chosen Vessels, take some time to journal your thoughts, to be quiet before the Lord, and to listen to Him. He will tell you that you are His child, and He will never leave you. Abba is calling, and He says, "Come unto Me, and I will give you rest, for My yoke is easy, and My burden is light" (Matthew 11:28-29, NKJV). When the time is right, spend time listening because God's revelation for your situation is forthcoming. You can sing your own song aloud unto the Lord based on your favorite Psalm.

QUESTIONS TO PONDER

God's Timing

1. Have you considered whether you really trust God for the purpose He has for your life?
2. How have your passions leveled during the past few months of tests and trials?
3. Are you willing to persevere in the deep waters of life?

What is your prayer today?

Journal

PRAYER THEME

Return to the Good Shepherd

Prayer Focus: Psalm 80:1-3, NKJV

Give ear, O Shepherd of Israel, You who lead Joseph like a flock; You who dwell *between* the cherubim, shine forth! Before Ephraim, Benjamin, and Manasseh, Stir up Your strength, And come *and* save us! Restore us, O God; Cause Your face to shine, And we shall be saved!

Prayer Focus Reflection

Several words may reign in your hearts today, and it is my belief that today's prayer focus is for us to ask God to rain on us by reviving and restoring our marriages and relationships. One may ask what it means to ask God to revive or restore. *Merriam Webster Dictionary* defines *revive* as *to make strong, healthy, or active again or to bring something back into use.* To *restore* means *to give back (someone or something that was lost or taken): to return (someone or something): to put or bring (something) back into existence or use.*

Psalm 80 allows your gifts to be stirred up. Ask Abba to stir up your gifts and speak aloud the following prayer to God.

Abba, we ask that You give ear, O Shepherd of Israel, help [us] to stop and listen to You as [we] walk this journey. Help [us] to stay connected to the vine because, as [our] vinedresser, You saved each of us in our wretchedness.

Lord, we ask that You revive and restore our families and marriages that the enemy is seeking to devour. Lord, restore us and smile upon us during darkness. Help us to walk in Your light and lead us to repentance when we realize we have done wrong. We thank You for hearing us and restoring us to our rightful place in Your presence.

Father, we bless You because only You can restore us. You are the only one that revives our hearts toward You. Dear Lord, thank You for granting us strength when we are weak. You, O Lord, have given us Your grace and restored us to You as our vinedresser. King of kings, allow us to walk in Your strength; as we encounter situations that aim to deplete us, we stand on Your Word, which will not return void (Isaiah 55:11, NJKV). Lord Jesus, we urgently exhort You or beg You to continue to rescue us by Your grace. We ask, dear Lord, that You please be merciful unto us. We repent from turning our hearts from You and ask You to restore what You have planted inside of us and return us to our first love, which is You.

Jesus, we ask You to cover any Chosen Vessel who is in a wayward relationship and save them, Lord. Please restore the love they once had for You. Help us not to settle for man's love, but to always seek Your agape love, dear Lord. We desire only You to restore (bring us back) to our rightful place where we belong. Lord, we speak of Your fruits, Your branches, and Your vine. Father, we thank You for repairing those of us who were broken when we began our walk with You. We thank You for our spiritual gift of helps. We hold on to John 15:5 (NKJV), that those of us who are connected to the vine can abide in our All-Powerful God and bear much fruit.

Thank You, Lord, for another opportunity to come before You, pray, and speak Your Word. We thank You for the spoken and written words of encouragement You have given us throughout the day. We ask You dear Lord to allow Your Words to become a Rhema Word in our lives. We ask You, Lord, to revive every situation that needs life. We ask that You restore broken relationships. We ask that You remove strife and any bitterness that we have been harboring. Please cast the resentment into the pit of hell and restore our joy as we call upon Your name.

Father, we close this prayer with a declaration of Your Word over our lives. We decree and declare that our lives will experience your goodness because of our connection to You as the Vine. We decree and declare that as you stirred up strength in Ephraim, Benjamin, and Manasseh, that You our all-Powerful God can stir up our strength and save us through Your anointing! Lord, help us to listen to You and commit to obey and surrender to Your way!

What has God revealed to you as you meditate on the scripture?

____

____

____

____

____

____

____

____

____

________________________________ *Journal*

QUESTIONS TO PONDER

Return to the Good Shepherd

1. Have you considered whether you really trust God for the purpose He has for your life?
2. How have your passions leveled during tests and trials you faced this past week?
3. Are you willing to persevere and go the distance even if you are feeling like a leaning or tottering wall?

What is your prayer today?

Journal

Pursuing Hope

Prayer Focus: Psalm 83:1-3, NKJV

Do not keep silent, O God! Do not hold Your peace, And do not be still, O God! For behold, Your enemies make a tumult; And those who hate You have lifted up their head. They have taken crafty counsel against Your people And consulted together against Your sheltered ones.

Prayer Focus Reflection

This is the day that the Lord has made; let us rejoice and be glad in it. Our God is an awesome God and I, like you, am glad to be united in holy fellowship and communion with Him. As you read the Scripture today, remember that the Lord meets us right where we were. As shared throughout our journey, the book of Psalms gives us instructions about how to deal with life.

Today's Scripture from Psalm 83 offers hope. God's Word is present. The Lord tells us that vengeance is His, so we are not to be ashamed or feel disgraced because He will do what He said He would do. He will destroy what is not right, and we just need to wait on Him. The enemy may conspire, but through seeking Him, we know His Word promises in Psalm 34:10b, "We shall not lack any good *thing*." He is our High Priest, and beside Him there is no other. He will take care of the enemy; we just need to be silent and still, and let Him destroy according to His precepts and time. We are God's Chosen Vessels.

Psalm 83 relates that war is forthcoming, and God protects His people. The Lord gave us examples in Deborah in Judges 4:4, Barak in Judges 4:6, and in the battle with Gideon in Judges 6:11. The Lord tells us in Psalm 83:13-14,

> Oh my God, make them like the whirling dust, Like the chaff before the wind! As the fire burns the woods, And as the flame sets the mountains on fire." (NKJV)

In Psalm 83:13, the winnowers had a job to do, just as we have a job to do in God's kingdom. The winnowers or fanners were the first to beat the kernels loose, and then they were to trample the kernels under foot to loosen the chaff or husk and separate it from the valuable grain. Do you want to be a winnower for the Lord? God has given us the ability to place our situations underfoot and watch the Lord separate the wheat from the chaff. The fanner had stages of winnowing, first with a five-or six-pronged pitchfork and a shovel for the second stage. Those things that were useless, would be blown away by the wind and burned. Is not that just like our God? He will move things out of the way and consume them or burn them, if you will. Allow the Lord to consume your situation, because you are God's valuable grain and God will separate what is true from what is false. Spend some time and learn more about the job of a winnower in Jeremiah 51:2; Ruth 3:2; Job 21:18; Psalm 1:4; Matthew 3:12; Isaiah 30:24; Jeremiah 23:28-29; and Luke 3:17.

Use God's Word as written in the Psalms to lead you on this journey of life; allow Him to handle your enemies according to His will. Don't carry shame, but speak peace. The Lord has set a time for your harvest, and He will send the wind to separate the wheat from the chaff.

Continue to draw close to Him by taking time to journal your thoughts, be quiet before the Lord, and allow Him to speak life gently into situations that appear to be dead. Remember that the second stage of winnowing requires a shovel. At times, you must bury the situation and cover it with God's love. Continue to allow the valuable grain to fall on good ground. Your harvest is coming!

What has God revealed to you as you meditate on the scripture?

Journal

QUESTIONS TO PONDER

Pursuing Hope

1. Have you considered God's purpose for your life today?
2. Have your passions yielded an excellent crop this day?
3. Are you willing to persevere as you till the soil within the surrounding areas of your life?

What is your prayer today?

Journal

PRAYER THEME

Prayer Focus: Psalm 88:1-3, NKJV

O Lord, God of my salvation, I have cried out day and night before You. Let my prayer come before You; Incline Your ear to my cry. For my soul is full of troubles, And my life draws near to the grave.

Prayer Focus Reflection

You know, the Lord ministers to us moment by moment and day by day. I am grateful for the way God speaks to us through His Word. Psalm 88 initially appeared to be a sad Psalm, but by reading and meditating on it, the Word of God revealed how the Lord used Heman the Ezrahite's pain and darkness to shed light for believers. Sometimes, believers may feel weighed down with emotional pain and non-believers may feel on the verge of losing control. The Lord wants us to be honest with ourselves because this is the best approach.

Psalm 88 speaks to both the believer and the non-believer. The believer has hope when praying, but the non-believer has no hope when praying until a connection and repentance take place. God inclines (bends or leans forward) His ear to our prayers when we are connected and in relationship with Him.

Prayer is communing and conversing with God. This can be done through spoken words, written words, thoughts, meditation, or song. God desires us to commune with Him, and prayer is our opportunity to do just that. Prayer is bi-directional, which means that we listen, but we also commune with God. God will speak to us through prayer, reading His Word, others who share His Word, our life circumstances, and His Holy Spirit.

Prayer is also defined as making a request known unto God through a petition that is made in a form of worship. This means we speak to God and commune with Him by worshipping Him, thanking Him, confessing to Him, and giving Him high praise as we adore Him. Chosen Vessels, let us pray God's Word to cover marriages, families, your community, and yourselves, be it in the workplace, in the home, or for our own mental and physical health. Our petitions and cries can spring forth as we pray. (Psalm 88:1-2, NKJV)

Let us pray:

Lord, we cry out and are thankful that we can bring our prayers before You, and that You will incline Your ear toward us. Lord, You give us hope as You listen for us to fill our moments of despondency or hopelessness with hope. Thank You, Lord, for waiting for us to cry out and offer us strength during our moments of feeling emotionally drained.

Dear Jesus, your Chosen Vessels bless You for inclining Your ear to our requests, our needs, and letting us know that through Your faithfulness, You reveal Your appointed time and remind us that You are always with us and will never leave us nor forsake us.

Father, You continue to remind us that no matter how weak our faith may be, that through Your grace, faithfulness, and hope, we can withstand. Your Word, anointing, and love toward us are faithful, and You offer us hope. You grant us a peace as we stand on Your Word and know without any doubt that You are always faithful toward us. We are grateful for the solid certainty that Your love offers us.

Almighty Savior, our being able to cry out to You gives us peace and a pathway to seek an answer from You during tough times. You hear our cry during our feelings of helplessness, You give us a strength that surpasses our understanding. You help us to stay afloat with Your Word and Your grace. Your Word serves as a lifejacket during life's storms. You as the All Sufficient One incline your ear to our cries, moment by moment, and time after time.

King of kings and Lord of lords, Your faithfulness restores us back to our place in You. You help us come back to our first love. Your faithfulness reminds us that we can submit to you and continue to fellowship with you in this journey; in You, we find a steady support!

Abba Father, at various moments in our lives when we looked back, we were not always in the best place; our thoughts were not always the best thoughts. However, You gave us the strength we needed to pull through. We may not be at the best place, but we are not in the worst place. We can say with Marvin Sapp, "I've made it through."

Lord Jesus, we are thankful for Your presence, which gives us hope. We thank You for leading and guiding us moment by moment and for surrounding our thoughts with love and grace toward our family and our communities.

Lord, even when we felt afflicted, we know that "weeping endures for a night, but joy comes in the morning" (Psalm 30:5)! By Your power, grace, and anointing, we can handle life's circumstances because You give us strength for the troubles and problems that beset us. Lord, Your peace surrounds our limited understanding, and we can have joy by trusting You!

All Sufficient One, no matter how dark the hour, how difficult the struggle, we can take joy in knowing that You are always present with us and around us through righteousness. You remind us in Psalm 37:6 that "[You] shall bring forth [Your] righteousness as the light and [Your] justice as the noonday."

Heavenly Father, we thank You for Your faithfulness, grace, and mercy. We ask that You continue to strengthen us when we are weak and bring discernment where there is confusion. Lord God, we ask for Your loving-kindness (tender and benevolent affection) to cover those dark periods in our lives. We decree and declare this evening that we will no longer dwell in darkness, but that we will arise in Your marvelous light! Lord, allow the floodgates of heaven to shower us with an abundance of rain on all relationships. Father, help us to become emotionally healthy; and when we are not, help us be honest and seek assistance from those you have made available to us, be it through professional help or spiritual counsel. Lord, we know that we are not alone, and we ask that You cover our minds with Your Word and drive out any darkness with Your mercy and faithfulness. Lord, help us to abide by Your Word as we walk this journey and confuse the enemy with our praise. It is in Your name that we pray, Amen!

QUESTIONS TO PONDER

A Prayer for Hope

1. Have you considered whether you really trust God for the purpose He has for your life?
2. What has been revealed about your passions during the past few months of test and trials?
3. Are you willing to persevere and go the distance no matter what?

What is your prayer today?

Journal

PRAYER THEME

The Servant's Promise

Prayer Focus: Psalm 89:1-3, NKJV

I will sing of the mercies of the Lord forever; With my mouth will I make known Your faithfulness to all generations. For I have said, "Mercy shall be built up forever; Your faithfulness You shall establish the very heavens." "I have made a covenant with My chosen, I have sworn to My servant David…"

Prayer Focus Reflection

Today may have appeared unsettling, disconnected, and even off course. You may have even been at a loss about what to say and even what to do. You may have received word from a loved one that rocked your confidence, shook your countenance, and even perplexed your mind. Does it seem like the enemy has you on lockdown? Remember you can decree and declare over yourself that your "greater" is coming. Speak aloud that the Lord is your help and your awesome God. Decree and declare your knowledge of Him as the author and finisher of your faith. Reflect throughout today that our Lord loves us so much that He gave us a promise.

As we look at Psalm 89, He promises to be with us always. If we incline our ears toward Him, He will speak when we listen. He tells us in Psalm

89:19 that He is our help. He tells us in Psalm 89:20 that He called us to be His servants. Servants sometimes get tired, and this is when you need to listen to your inner voice and become still in your situation. God tells us in Psalm 89:21 that He is our strength, so be not weary, because our Lord's anointing and healing virtues are all around us.

When we take time daily to pray, the enemy will throw fiery darts. But know the devil is a liar! Prayer is an offensive weapon, and a daily prayer life teaches us that we can overcome any obstacle(s) through prayer. Do not worry, Chosen Vessels, because God has promised us in Psalm 89:21 that His hand is with us. We are His faithful servants, and He will give us freedom from our affliction as stated in Psalm 89:22. We are not to be deceived because our God is not mocked. He says in Psalm 89:22 that He will free us from deception. The enemy will try to deceive us, but our focus is on God's anointing over our lives. Our focus from this day forward should be to continue to meditate on God's Word day and night.

See, Chosen Vessels, the devil knows that if he can distract us and divert our focus to the problem, then we would attempt to resolve it in our own strength; but we know that we have the victory over the enemy and his tactics. God says in Psalm 89:23 that he has given us the victory! Many of us can testify without a shadow of doubt to God being faithful, and He is kind, as He reminds us in Psalm 89:24. He influences the world according to Psalm 89:25. He has saving power over anyone who is out of fellowship with Abba Father. Check out God's Word in Psalm 89:26, He promises to be our saving power. His Word is so awesome.

These few passages of Scripture give us foundational principles to use in standing true to His Word. When we do, then God's anointing will overshadow us, and that leads us right into Psalm 90:1-2;

> Lord, You have been our dwelling place in all generations. Before the mountains were brought forth, Or ever You had formed the earth and the world, Even from everlasting to everlasting, You *are* God.

Chosen Vessels, the Lord knows our state, and it has been declared over us that faithfulness is the road we shall travel. We shall remain loyal to God's Word and His way, which is the pathway we are to follow. Therefore, let us continue to study to show ourselves approved. Let us continue to talk to God when we feel helpless and hopeless. Let us not forget His benefits and the power of reading His Word. Let us hide the Word in our hearts and continue to bless Him for giving us the book of Psalms as a guidebook for our lives. Let us read the next passages of Scripture with expectation and allow the Lord to give us rest so we can become refreshed, replenished and have a greater focus on the anointing He has given to each of us and follow the biblical instructions as we walk this life's journey.

Let us continue to get so close to Him that His anointing will saturate us. As we journal our thoughts and become quiet in His presence, our situations will start changing because of how we have positioned ourselves. We will hear with such clarity and gain such discernment because His voice says, Psalm 27:14,

> Wait on [Me] and be of good courage, and [I] will strengthen your hearts, wait I say on [Me].

Allow Him to gently speak life to your situation and be okay with waiting to hear His voice. Remember God's revelation for our situation is forthcoming as we spend time with Him.

QUESTIONS TO PONDER

The Servant's Promise

1. Have you considered whether you really trust God for the purpose He has for your life?
2. What has been revealed about your passions during today's tests and trials?
3. Are you willing to persevere and go the distance no matter what?

What is your prayer today?

Journal

PRAYER THEME

Worship is Our Security from God

Prayer Focus: Psalm 95:1-3, NKJV

Oh come, let us sing to the LORD! Let us shout joyfully to the Rock of our salvation. Let us come before His presence with thanksgiving; Let us shout joyfully to Him with psalms. For the Lord *is* the great God, And the great King above all gods.

Prayer Focus Reflection

Thank You, Lord, for Chosen Vessels Pray. Thank you for the ministering words spoken to us throughout today. Thank You for reminding us of Your desire for us to come, reminding us of our need to spend time with You, and reminding us of our ability to worship You in spirit and in truth. Thank You for letting us know that as we yield to Your voice and surrender unto Your way, we can be safe in You.

The themes of Psalm 95 are worship and praise. God is inviting us as His people to come and worship Him. This ministry of Psalm 95 helps us as believers to reflect in our hearts on the service of worship. God requires us to set our hearts and attention toward Him. When we focus on God and address worship, we can walk in obedience and receive salvation from God who is our solid Rock.

Psalm 95:5, 6, and 7 (Contemporary English Version):

> The ocean is the Lord's because he made it, and with his own hands, he formed the dry land. Bow down and worship the Lord our Creator! The Lord is our God and we are his people, the sheep he takes care of in his own pasture.

As we extol the Lord and proclaim Him greater than any problems we have, we can sing unto the Lord. Psalm 95 serves as a conditional praise for us. By singing, we worship the Lord in humble submission and adoration (meaning we make God the center and focus on His greatness).

Let us begin to open our mouths and worship God for His continual support to us:

Father, we thank You for Your hand, which continually supports and helps us. We thank You for the numerous times when You remind us that we can come at Your invitation and that we are to invite others.

Father, we thank You for the opportunity for allowing us to come before You with thanksgiving. We acknowledge that Your grace is the reason we made it another day. We bless You for hearing our cry. Thank You for whispering in our ear and bidding us to come closer unto You. We are guided by Your voice and committed to surrender unto Your will. We aim to follow You, dear Lord, in Your path of righteousness. We kneel in surrender unto You, Abba Father. We will move at Your command and travel Your path of righteousness. We will draw ourselves closer to Your way. We will draw unto You, dear Shepherd, as the one who speaks to our soul.

You, Lord, are a great God and King. There is no one like You. We thank You for reminding us of Your greatness and reminding us that You are above all things. We thank You for reminding us that sheep are not dumb, but they are needy. We want a closer relationship with You every day and place our purpose in Your hand. We thank You that we can place our doubts into the sea of forgetfulness, because You are our Shepherd, and we shall not want.

It is God's Word that gives us joy and You who gives us life. Your Word upholds our family, our spouses, our children, and our circumstances. You hold our concerns in Your hands, and therefore we offer a prayer of thanksgiving to You, God, for Your grace, love, mercy, and favor. We thank You, God, for giving Your only begotten Son so that whosoever believes in You will not perish but shall have everlasting life (John 3:16, NKJV).

We close this prayer, dear Lord, by honoring You because You are worthy to be praised. We thank You, Father, for this day and for allowing us to get to know You in a more intimate way. We are committing to study Your Word more, so we can know You better for ourselves. Father, we ask that You allow an abundance of rain to fall upon our lives, so we may flourish and advance in You.

Lord, help us to worship You in Spirit and in Truth, as we walk this journey of life! In Your name, Jesus, the Chosen Vessels Pray, Amen and Amen!

QUESTIONS TO PONDER

Worship is Our Security from God

1. What is the purpose of worship, and how can you focus more on worshipping Him?
2. If the Lord had not been on your side, where do you think your passions would lie?
3. Are you willing to remain steadfast and unmovable during profound changes in your life?

What is your prayer today?

Journal

PRAYER THEME

Remember God's Got It

Prayer Focus: Psalm 102:1-3, NKJV

Hear my prayer, O LORD, And let my cry come to You. Do not hide Your face from me in the day of trouble; Incline Your ear to me; In the day that I call, answer me speedily. For my days are consumed like smoke, And my bones are burned like a hearth.

Prayer Focus Reflection

God's spoken Word reminds us that He is with us in every season of life. Thank Him for reminding us that even in the worst times we are too blessed to be stressed. His Word grants us a peace that surpasses our understanding. Our God still reigns at every point of our lives, and what the Lord requires of us is obedience. In Psalm 102:1-11, the Psalmist highlights the moaning and groaning as sorrowful experiences. However, Psalm 102:12-28 speaks to better things coming.

As the Lord's Chosen Vessels, He places His anointing all around us. We must begin with the word *trust*. We are to trust God through the storms of life. Because He is an unchanging God, we can take joy in knowing that He has us in the palm of His hands. God has given us grace to know that we will influence the generations to come, so we want to continue to endure even in the midst of our groaning. Our Lord is the same and He changes not. He is faithful and sovereign; He is with us. The Lord assures us that He hears our prayers and will listen to us.

Call out unto the Lord and give Him back His Word:

We open this prayer, dear Lord, by honoring You because You are worthy to be praised. We thank You for this day and for allowing us to get to know You in a more intimate way as we study to show ourselves approved, read Thy Word and hide it in our hearts, and allow it to become oil to be shared with our families. We are committing to study Your Word more, so we can know You better for ourselves. Father, we ask that You allow an abundance of rain to fall upon our lives, so we may flourish to advance Your kingdom. Lord, help us to worship You in Spirit and in Truth as we walk this journey of life as Your vessels of honor! In Your name, Jesus, the Chosen Vessels Pray, Amen and Amen!

What has God revealed to you as you meditate on the scripture?

____

____

____

____

____

____

____

____

____

________________________________ *Journal*

QUESTIONS TO PONDER

Remember God's Got It

1. Have you considered whether you really trust God for the purpose; do you really believe that God's got it—that He has your situation under control?

2. What has been revealed to you about your "it" and your passions at this very moment?

3. Are you willing to persevere and go the distance no matter what?

What is your prayer today?

Journal

PRAYER THEME

Grateful Worship

Prayer Focus: Psalm 116:1-3, NKJV

I love the LORD, because He has heard My voice and my supplications. Because He has inclined His ear to me, Therefore I will call upon Him as long as I live. The pains of death surrounded me, And the pangs of Sheol laid hold of me; I found trouble and sorrow.

Prayer Focus Reflection

Thank the Lord for reconfirming our vows and commitment to be better disciples for God's kingdom business. There is power in prayer. Today's Scripture reminds us that the Lord loves us, hears us, and answers our prayers. As we express our thanks to the Lord, we are consistently reminded in God's Word that God is moved by our words of praise, and He loves to be in fellowship with us. Psalm 116: 4-7 and Psalm 116:16-18 are also part of today's Scripture focus.

As the Lord's Chosen Vessels, God speaks to us through Psalm 116, which is a song of thanksgiving and a commitment to personally call upon the Lord. Praying seals our commission to remain faithful to the Lord. As we pray God's Word, we reflect on the need for compassion and rest. We are reminded by God's Word that He uses situations to place us in the center of His care. We see that nothing is too small for us to talk to God about.

The Lord gives us opportunities to seek His face and cry out to Him for what only He can give us. God honors the vows we make, and there are benefits to having a relationship with the Lord. When we pray, we are to call upon the name of the Lord and offer sacrifices of thanksgiving unto our Lord. We are to continually praise God and thank Him no matter the circumstances because He will supply our every need.

Sometimes, we may not understand why we are placed in certain situations, but the Lord knows what we need. However, in some seasons of our lives, we need to stand still, rest in Him, and see the salvation of the Lord. The Lord teaches us to place our confidence in Him and to totally depend on God and not ourselves, even when we are independent women. Independent women need God more because the enemy can use our independent spirit to lead us astray.

Prayer enables us to connect with our Maker and have a more intimate relationship with Him. Our connection to one another holds us accountable to live the way God desires us to live and walk on this Christian journey.

Let us offer a prayer of supplication unto God:

Lord, we honor You for Your faithfulness toward us. We thank You, Father, for this day and for allowing us to understand that You really hear us and listen to us. Father, during our distress, You give us the ability to call out unto You. Lord, Your Word highlights Your goodness and Your mercy. Your Word supplies us a cup of salvation, and when we fulfill our vow, You open the windows of heaven and pour out a blessing.

Lord, we desire to serve You continually and offer a thank offering unto You because You have "inclined your ear to us" (Psalm 116:2). Father, we ask You to help us to fulfill our vows and take time each day to seal our hearts with Your Word and to remember that our connections serve as stepping stones to someone learning about You as they read and pray Your Word. Allow us, Lord, to read a Psalm each day; pour Your Word all over our minds, and as we partake of Your Word, help us to commit to living a more victorious life in You. Father, in this season of life, we are asking for an abundance of rain that will bring forth a harvest of believers to know the truth, so they can be free. Lord, help us worship You, praise You, and walk this journey in peace, passion, and faith, surrounded by Your grace as Your vessels of honor!

What has God revealed to you as you meditate on the scripture?

Journal

QUESTIONS TO PONDER

Grateful Worship

1. Have you considered whether you really have included worship as part of your purpose-filled life?
2. What has been revealed about your passion for worshipping God always?
3. Are you willing to persevere and go the distance no matter what?

What is your prayer today?

Journal

PRAYER THEME

Looking for God

Prayer Focus: Psalm 123:1-3, NKJV

Unto You I lift up my eyes, O You who dwell in the heavens. Behold, as the eyes of servants *look* to the hand of their masters, As the eyes of a maid to the hand of her mistress, So our eyes *look* to the LORD our God until He has mercy on us. Have mercy on us. O LORD, have mercy on us! For we are exceedingly filled with contempt.

Prayer Focus Reflection

I bless the Lord for His Word, which is a light unto our path. This Psalm speaks about lifting up our eyes, which helped me to look a little deeper. When one thinks of the eye, several thoughts come to mind. Some have said the eyes are the windows to the soul. Others think about focus. Do you need to refocus on some things? Have you allowed your situation to distract you from God's purpose for your life? I like what the Life Application Bible says about this Psalm. The commentator asks where your concentration lies. Are you concentrating on God with a steadfast devotion and expectation? When we hear that it is going to rain or snow, we look up to the sky. This is exactly what the Lord wants us to do—to look up to the hills, from whence cometh our help. We are to fix our eyes on the Lord because He is our hope.

Today's Scripture centers our eyes on the Lord. Eyes are defined as a part of the body that can see; and from the eyes, we are able to understand and appreciate something that is seen. To dwell means to remain for a time or to live or exist. Where do you allow your eyes to dwell? Psalm 123:2 tells us to,

> Behold, as the eyes of servants look to the hand of their masters, As the eyes of a maid to the hand of her mistress, So our eyes look to the Lord our God, Until He has mercy on us.

As the Lord's Chosen Vessels, God speaks to us through His Word. Psalm 123 is a short but powerful song. It is helping us to stay focused on our Maker and setting our sights on Him! Through God's Word, we can gaze upon Him, observe, and perceive an understanding. As God's servants, God gave us an anointing to perform His duties and help to guide people. As we direct our attention to the Lord, we help others gain their personal power to own the hidden treasure God's relationship offers. Chosen Vessels, let us direct our eyes to the very place on which the Lord wants us to focus. As you reflect on this passage of Scripture, look to God for help. Keep your eyes upon Him. Do not let your focus be on things that are not of God; put yourself in a posture of thankfulness. Thank Him for His mercy and grace over you.

Let us pray:

Father, we look to You, our heaven-dwelling God, for help. Merciful God, thank You for helping us to look for a positive/helpful response when we encounter contempt in our home and community. We bless You and thank You, Lord. Our eyes are waiting upon You, dear Lord. We cover our natural and spiritual family in prayer. Lord, deliver us from contempt that causes us to focus on disobedience. Father, thank You for strength. Thank You for Your mercy and grace over us as our Sustainer as we go through issues and struggles. Thank You, Lord, for guiding and showing us how to continue to walk upright before You, God, as we commit our way to You. You promised to give us the desires of our heart as we walk upright before You. We want those desires to honor and to bring glory to You, Lord, because You are our Keeper and way maker. You are the Author and Finisher of our faith.

We lift You up as in the song of ascent that focuses on the children of Israel in their journey to go up and worship You, O God. Let us each continue to look up to You, our Abba Father who art in heaven. Father, we look to You for healing. We look to You for restoring our relationships. We look to You to encourage families during storms. Father, we thank You for words of encouragement that help us along the way as we make this journey of life.

We close this prayer, Lord, by honoring You for enabling us to see ourselves. We thank You, Father, for this day and for allowing us to understand the power of worshiping You in spirit and in truth. Father, during our lack of focus and areas of contempt, give us the ability to call out unto You for mercy and deliverance. Lord, Your Word highlights Your goodness and mercy toward us. Lord, please open the eyes of our hearts, so we may see You.

Father, in this season of life, allow our eyes to remain focused so that we can bring all the glory and honor unto You. Help us worship You, focus on Your purpose, and walk this journey in peace, mercy, and grace as God's vessels of honor! In Your name, Jesus, the Chosen Vessels Pray, Amen and Amen!

QUESTIONS TO PONDER

Looking for God

1. Have you considered whether you really will look to the hills from where your help comes about the purpose God has for your life?

2. What has been revealed about your passions concerning the goodness of God?

3. Are you willing to persevere and go the distance no matter what?

What is your prayer today?

Journal

PRAYER THEME

The Chosen Vessel "If"

Prayer Focus: Psalm 124:1-3, NKJV

"If it had not been the LORD who was on our side," Let Israel now say – "If it had not been the LORD who was on our side, When men rose up against us, Then they would have swallowed us alive, When their wrath was kindled against us;

Prayer Focus Reflection

When you read the word *if*, what comes to mind? Well, according to *Merriam Webster Dictionary*, the word means:

> In the event that, allowing that, on the assumption that, on condition that, whether, used as a function to introduce, even though and even saying perhaps.

Each of the words listed above confirm that "if" we as God's people continue to humble ourselves and do what the Lord has called us to do, we can remain confident because we know to whom we belong, and we know that the Lord has our back. Let us take a few minutes and ponder on this Scripture and on the words that stand out. As we do, write down a goal for this day about where you desire to grow in God's grace. Allow the kindling of God's anointing to refresh the fire within you. Allow God's Word to cover your situation, knowing that only He can rekindle and restore.

Remind yourself to look forward and upward and know that He knows when a sparrow falls, and He knows when the enemy seeks to steal, kill, and destroy you; but he cannot because God has given us a way to escape. As Psalm 124:7 says,

> Our soul has escaped as a bird from the snare of the fowlers,
> the snare is broken, and we have escaped.

Because the Lord is on our side, the snare (the entanglements or the difficulties) are broken and *if God* had not been on our side, we would not have a way of escape. Therefore, Chosen Vessels, our God has given us His signed, sealed and delivered "get out of jail free card." We could have been swallowed up alive and without hope, but we can bless God that He gave us a way of escape and He will strengthen us, heal us, protect us, and guide us in our *if* situations.

In reflecting on Psalm 124 in sections, look at how battles come into our lives. During the battle, we must put on our war clothes. So, Chosen Vessels, prepare for your battle and know that we have the victory! Let us put on our helmet of salvation to cover our minds because, just as the Israelites feared being swallowed up alive, the enemy's wrath being kindled against them, the waters overwhelming them and the stream overwhelming their souls, they blessed God during their *if* reflection or situation. See, we can take joy in knowing that we do not have to worry about *if* the Lord will be there with us. He said He would never leave us nor forsake us.

So *if* the enemy seeks to distract or entrap us, we can bless God all the more because, in our difficulties or circumstances, our Sword of the Spirit can strike down the enemy, our breastplate of righteousness gives us protection for our heart, our loins girded with truth give us a way of escape. God's Word is true, and it never fails. Let us put our feet in His gospel of peace.

Are you ready to place God's marker of Psalm 124 on the battle of your mind, tongue, heart, soul, job, marriage, or relationships? We can take joy in knowing that God is on our side, and we know where we would be *if* He did not lead us!

QUESTIONS TO PONDER

The Chosen Vessel "If"

1. Have you considered where you would be if God's purpose for your life was not already planned?
2. What has been revealed about your passions toward your family, your friends, and your foes?
3. Are you willing to persevere and go the distance no matter what?

What is your prayer today?

Journal

PRAYER THEME

Being Still During Weighty Matters

Prayer Focus: Psalm 131:1-3, NKJV

LORD, my heart is not haughty, Nor my eyes lofty. Neither do I concern myself with great matters, Nor with things too profound for me. Surely, I have calmed and quieted my soul, Like a weaned child with his mother; Like a weaned child *is* my soul within me. O Israel, hope in the LORD From this time forth and forever.

Prayer Focus Reflection

The focus word of this Psalm is *trust*, and today it speaks volumes about the noise in life and how many times we fall into a trap of displaying a prideful spirit. Immediately seeking God's forgiveness can quiet the spirit as well as open the eyes of one's heart. With a quiet spirit and opened eyes, then we can see Him. Our desire, Chosen Vessels, should be to walk in hope, stillness, and quietness.

As we cast our concerns on the Lord, we must begin by laying bitterness, financial concerns, marital woes, trust, anxiety, depression, and negative thoughts right on God's altar. Once we release the load, we will experience a peace that surpasses our understanding.

Now, Chosen Vessels, reread Psalm 131 very slowly prior to going to bed today. Pull out your journal, take some time, and imagine if you will that your soul represents a child on your lap. Imagine the fussiness that happens when a nursing child is hungry and thirsty. Begin to ask yourself a few questions:

- † Have today and the past few days seemed like a nursing child waiting to latch on to be fed, but you are all dried up and have no milk to offer?
- † Has this day been fueled with fear, rejection, and utter despair?

Write your responses and know that the Lord chose today to let us know that He is willing to quiet our souls with His peace that surpasses our understanding if we will just be still and allow His Word to serve as milk to a hungry and fussy soul. Sometimes we become so hurried, and we just need to pause for a moment and bask in the stillness of God.

So, stop, lay down your pen, settle your soul, and listen attentively to these passages of Scripture as we quietly reflect on this short passage and write on the tables of our hearts. Think about what God is saying to you right now. Then, pick up your pen and write for the next sixty seconds what you hear the Lord speaking to your soul. Don't be concerned about spelling, punctuation, or what you're writing, just write down what you are hearing during this stillness as God feeds you with His Word.

QUESTIONS TO PONDER

Being Still During Weighty Matters

1. What is the purpose of being still before the Lord?
2. What passions have stirred your soul during those weighty matters?
3. Are you willing to persevere and go the distance no matter how "fussy" life circumstances become?

What is your prayer today?

Journal

PRAYER THEME

Enter God's Chamber

Prayer Focus: Psalm 132:1-3, NKJV

Lord, remember David *And* all his afflictions; How he swore to the Lord, *And* vowed to the Mighty One of Jacob: "Surely I will not go into the chamber of my house, Or go up to the comfort of my bed..."

Prayer Focus Reflection

I really love studying and praying God's Word. I am so excited about how God enables us to get back to the basics and pray. Connecting with other Chosen Vessels enables us to grow in God's grace. A simple request to God is honored and answered. As God has shared with us throughout our time together that Psalms speak of worship, this praise book and common book of prayer conditions our hearts to worship Abba Father. God's Word offers us a renewed commitment and guidance in our daily walk. As we pray the Psalms, we become refined and better because of God's Word. From the Word of God, we can experience and encounter the full mercy of our God.

Today's prayer focus is Psalm 132:5-8; verse 7 stood out to me: "Let us go into the tabernacle; Let us worship at His footstool." The Ark of the Covenant (tabernacle or testimony) made of acacia wood symbolizes the covenant relationship between God and His people. This was not an ordinary piece of furniture. This furniture reminded God's people of God's will and their duty. The tablets of the law are called the Testimony, and people are to obey God. The top of the Ark represented God's mercy seat, and this seat was between the witness and the presence of the Lord. Blood would be sprinkled once a year (Leviticus 16:2, 14-16) as an atonement that made possible forgiveness of sin and continual communion between God and the people. I see the advantage of being at the feet of Jesus and bowing down in worship, for His mercy redeems us.

Our closing prayer:

Father, Your sacrifice is our center. Your love places Your Spirit within each of us. Lord, we are coming to You on behalf of those who have important life decisions to make, who feel the pain is unbearable and the current state of affairs is not sustainable. Lord, I hear You speaking and saying to my sisters, "Arise, you have laid it at My feet!" Thank you, Lord, for allowing Your grace to cover their minds, Your anointing to arise within them, and Your peace to go ahead of them in the coming days.

Please allow us to see Your mighty hand change these situations in their lives to close the gap(s). Father, we will glorify Your name and commit to spend time with You daily. Your everlasting Word keeps our soul alive and at perfect peace. We bless You, Lord, for the boldness that You have given us. We thank You for Your sacrifice and love toward us. Our lives are sufficient because of Your grace, mercy, peace, and anointing dwells in each of us. Thank You for loving us, Amen.

God's Word energizes and enlightens our lives. God's presence is illuminating and restoring each time we spend time studying, reading, and obeying His Word. As we take time daily to spend quality time with God, we are equipping ourselves to be better students and Ambassadors for His kingdom. Let us continue to hold fast to a "Yes, I will trust and obey God." His favor and anointing beckons us to move forward in His grace, truth, and freedom.

QUESTIONS TO PONDER

Enter God's Chamber

1. Have you considered if the perceived gaps you hold have held you back from fulfilling God's purpose in your life?
2. How have your passions leveled during the gaps in your life?
3. Are you willing to persevere and go the distance to close any gaps, no matter what?

What is your prayer today?

Journal

PRAYER THEME

His Mercy Endures Forever

Prayer Focus: Psalm 136:1-3, NKJV

Oh, give thanks to the LORD, for *He* is good! For His mercy *endures* forever. Oh, give thanks to the God of gods! For His mercy *endures* forever. Oh, give thanks to the Lord of lords! For His mercy *endures* forever.

Prayer Focus Reflection

Today's prayer focus really allows each of us to reflect on God's love toward us. I love how God's Word ushers us into His presence each day. It is clear how much the Lord inhabits the praises of His people. When we study, read, and pray God's Word, we are daily expressing our love to the Lord, our Savior, God, healer, and redeemer. Jesus' spoken word in Matthew 22:37-38 expresses that the greatest commandment is that we love Him with all our heart, soul, and mind. Psalm 136 helps us learn how to love God and worship Him. Through His Word, God allows us to express our deepest thoughts and allows His Word to bring healing and redemption to our souls. We should lay any feelings of despair at the feet of Jesus. We should stand on His Word and give thanks to the Lord, for He is good. (Psalm 136:1, NKJV)

The Psalms are called the "songs of praise" in Hebrew. The prayers in the book of Psalms highlight every emotion from our feelings about our life's journey. In addition, these "songs of praise" unveil our attitude toward life. Through the readings and reflections of God's Word found in this Psalm, we can learn firsthand how character defines who you are. *Character* is defined as *the inward values that determines outward actions*. Our prayers to God express our inward feelings and attitudes of life, from the dark periods to times of praise and joy. As we read aloud, pray aloud, sing aloud, and reflect on various passages in Psalms, we can spend some time reflecting on our character, but also really seeking God and surrendering to Him. Our time with Him helps us to allow God to conduct an inquiry on us. He will look deep within our hearts, so that He can find out everything we are thinking, feeling, and hoping for as we walk this journey of life.

Several songs may speak to your heart today; play those songs that come to mind and reflect on His goodness toward you. It is so true that God knows the plans He has for us (Jeremiah 29:11). Our desire is to ask God to grant us an outpouring of His Spirit, holiness, and grace to spread all over us. Think about the Lord's goodness and thank Him for how His blessings as well as reading Scripture prompts us to want Him more than anything.

Therefore, Chosen Vessels, God's Word spoke to us in Psalm 136 on the benefits of giving God thanks because "God's love never fails, and His mercy endures forever."

Let us aim to be the vessels that God has called us to be and set our thoughts toward praising Him with all our hearts. We know so well that God's love never fails, and we should be like the deer and allow our heart to pant after God. We should praise God and thank Him for keeping us, restoring us, embracing us, loving us, and forgiving us. Do you need to make some good decisions? Listen to inspirational words of wisdom from Spirit-led teachers. Find time to listen to songs of worship.

As you set aside a time of worship, you will see how God's Word energizes and enlightens our lives daily. God's presence is illuminating and restoring each time we spend time studying, reading, and basking in His anointed Word. As we take time daily to spend quality time with God, we are equipping ourselves to be better students of His Word so that we can share the Gospel of Jesus Christ as His ambassadors for His kingdom. Let us continue to hold fast to a "Yes, I will trust and obey God." His favor and anointing beckons us to move forward in His grace, truth, and freedom.

Let us pray:
Father, we thank You for Your sacrifice and love toward us. Our lives are sufficient because Your grace, mercy, peace, and anointing dwells in each of us. Thank You, dear Lord, for loving us, Amen.

What has God revealed to you as you meditate on the scripture?

Journal

QUESTIONS TO PONDER

His Mercy Endures Forever

1. Have you considered whether you really are willing to trust and obey God for the purposes He outlines for your life?
2. How have your passions leveled during this season of your life?
3. Are you willing to persevere, trust and obey God as you go the distance?

What is your prayer today?

Journal

Speaking the Bitter Truth

Prayer Focus: Psalm 137:1-3, NKJV

By the rivers of Babylon, There we sat down, yea, we wept When we remembered Zion. We hung our harps Upon the willows in the midst of it. For there those who carried us away captive asked of us a song, And those who plundered us *requested* mirth, *Saying*, "Sing us *one* of the songs of Zion!"

Prayer Focus Reflection

The purpose of Psalm 137 speaks to how Judah fell to its enemy, the Babylonians, who then destroyed most of the survivors. In the Psalm, Jeremiah, who is believed to be the author according to Rabbinical sources, highlights how Judah reflected on those bitter days of captivity and cried out for justice. The Lord meets us during our pain and grants us His sustaining power, and He will help us during our pain spiritually, emotionally, and physically.

Babylon was a foreign land, and God's people were sorrowful, to the point that they were unwilling to sing. The Lord requires us to be real about our feelings; that is the only way for our deliverance to happen. It does not good to hide our feelings, no matter how ugly they may seem to be; the Lord knows our innermost thoughts.

In Psalm 137, the Israelites brought their anger, disappointment, and pain to God. From my perspective, the Lord gave us an actual account of what raw emotion looks like when the children of Judah were in bondage. This offers us some encouragement, as they were honest about how they felt, just as we are to be also. It is healthy to express feelings of agony; such expression leads to healing.

Psalm 137 summarizes for us of how the children of Israel were so despondent as to be unable to worship the Lord in a foreign land. Oh, but God taught the children of Israel how to worship Him no matter where they were, and He also used their isolation to manifest His plans for them to introduce Jesus to the Greeks. Scripture says that they cried on the riverbanks of Babylon (137:1). They could not understand how their captors wanted them to sing songs of Zion while their beloved city was laid waste (Psalm 137:3). Some define worship as us taking an opportunity to really express ourselves to God with honesty, no matter how ugly it happens to be. God is not swayed by the many ins and outs we encounter emotionally because He knows all about us. Nor does He not want us to be honest. He wants to deliver us from the poison that lurks inside of us. We have a personal invitation to be real before the Lord, as He has given us authority to come boldly to His mighty throne of grace.

True worship involves speaking truth that expresses our real feelings, no matter how dark our emotions may be. The Lord judges our heart. In our disclosure, we should listen to our "Abba" Father so we can incline our ears to hear what the Lord has to say in return. Burying emotions and thoughts yields only despair. God desires us to cast our cares on Him, for He cares for us.

The Lord said in Psalm 136 that God's mercy endures forever. The Babylonians asked the children of Judah to sing a song. Truth reveals the enemy, and a song of praise can diffuse the enemy. God's love has the power to uproot dark emotions and allow us to walk in God's peace and understanding. Therefore, Chosen Vessels, let us express our emotions and speak TRUTH:

† **T**reasure the stillness with the Lord.

† **R**eflect on how His love never quits.

† **U**nlock the uncertainty within you and

† **T**hrough God's Word let Him give you songs of praise.

† **H**old fast to His Word as His mercy endures forever.

Expressing our true emotions will help us during times of pain, frustrations, lack of trust, and uncertainty. Through God's Word, we can see where our help lies, and our help comes from the Lord. He will lead us and guide us into all truth.

Let us pray:
Lord, we honor You this day for enabling us to cry out to You for help from the depths of our soul.

What has God revealed to you as you meditate on the scripture?

____

____

____

____

____

____

____

____

___________________________________ *Journal*

QUESTIONS TO PONDER

Speaking the Bitter Truth

1. Have you considered if your bouts of bitterness have hindered God's purpose for your life?
2. What has been revealed about your lack of passion because of ongoing bouts of bitterness?
3. Are you willing to persevere and go the distance and release the bitterness?

What is your prayer today?

Journal

PRAYER THEME

The Awakening of the Ministry of Prayer

Prayer Focus: Psalm 138:1-3, NKJV

I will praise You with my whole heart; Before the gods I will sing praises to You. I will worship toward Your holy temple, And praise Your name For Your lovingkindness and Your truth; For You have magnified Your word above all Your name. In the day when I cried out, You answered me *And* made me bold *with* strength in my soul.

Prayer Focus Reflection

God's Word is ever true; His mercy endures forever. Going forward, expect the unexpected as God's supernatural anointing covers us. Humble yourselves and listen attentively to what the Lord is whispering in your ears and speaking to your hearts in the days to come. Once your ministry of prayer is awakened and your gift stirred, you will begin to hear with greater clarity what the Lord is speaking to you. Write down what He says and continue to pray to Abba Father. The Lord will hear your cry and reward you for your faithfulness through reaping what Abba has for you. If you sow good seeds and water them through a season of prayer, you will reap a harvest designed and ordained by God.

The Lord will speak to each of us in a manner that is linked to our relationship with Him. To some, He will speak in an audible voice to our souls. For others, He will allow His Words to leap off the pages of Scripture. Some are to write and not put down your pen until He tells you because He is speaking to you through your writings. God will fulfill our purpose in our lives, and we will be His salt to the earth (Matthew 5:13, NKJV).

Psalm 138:7-8 (CEV),

> "Though I walk in the midst of trouble, you preserve my life; you stretch out your hand against the wrath of my enemies, and your right hand delivers me. The Lord will fulfill his purpose for me; your steadfast love, O Lord, endures forever. Do not forsake the work of your hands."

Chosen Vessels, when we are doing what God has purposed for us to do, that is when we need help. We are to call unto the Lord and He will answer us (Jeremiah 33:3). The Lord has promised to be with us in our time of need and trouble.

Chosen Vessels, many are following a false god, but our purpose is to bring clarity to the souls we encounter on this journey. Psalm 138:1-5 speaks of God as everything. He is our everything. He is our keeper. He is our way maker. He is our hope. He is our redeemer. He is our king. He is our Lord. He is our healer. He is our sovereign one. He is our Lord. He is the lover of our soul! The Lord is our all in all. He wants us to walk in our anointing and share our testimonies.

QUESTIONS TO PONDER

The Awakening of the Ministry of Prayer

1. What is the purpose of prayer during this season of revival?
2. Has your passion of prayer been awakened?
3. Are you committed to persevere and take part in this revival of prayer throughout the land?

What is your prayer today?

Journal

PRAYER THEME

God's Support In Battle

Prayer Focus: Psalm 144:1-3, NKJV

Blessed *be* the LORD my Rock, Who trains my hands for war, *And* my fingers for battle—My lovingkindness and my fortress, My high tower and my deliverer, My shield and *the One* in whom I take refuge, Who subdues my people under me. LORD, what *is* man, that You take knowledge of him? *Or* the son of man, that You are mindful of him?

Prayer Focus Reflection

The purpose of Psalm 144 speaks to our praising God for being with us during battles…in marriages, illnesses, death, financial challenges, inappropriate relationships, and other issues that produce a lack of trust. Some battles occur in the mind during our seeking to be God's Chosen Vessels. The Lord is telling us not to look at victory through the eyes of man. We are not to put our trust in troops, technology, or some cunning strategy that may come to mind. We are to rely on the Lord and put our confidence and trust in Him.

In Psalm 144, David learned how worthiness hinges on his relationship with God. When God sees us, He sees the blood of Jesus, and this places us in a proper stance with God, as Psalm 144 displays humility. In Matthew 22:37-38, Jesus said that the greatest commandment was to love the Lord with all our heart, soul, and mind. Through the Psalms, we are invited to come worship as well as serve Him. The global message is that we are to worship the Lord in spirit and in truth. Even with David being a man after God's own heart, David needed Jesus as his Lord; once David surrendered his will and submitted his heart to his ruler, this enabled David to give voice to his spirit. We, too, have an opportunity to lift our hearts to the Lord.

When entering a battle, our prayer is:

Dear Lord, Your Chosen Vessels come to You today to say thank You. We bless You for Your Word and thank You for letting us know that, when we enter a battle, be it in mind or in circumstance, You, O Lord, have trained us to fight fair and well. You, O Lord, have trained us to love family, friends, and foes. Thank You, Father, for training us to resist the devil's attacks against us.

You, oh Lord, have given us Your favor and protection. You have been and will continue to be our rock and our refuge. You have been so mindful toward us, and we are grateful for Your supplying us with a godly happiness. Lord, our life is just a vapor or breath that shall pass like a shadow, but we decree and declare that we will lift [our] eyes to the hills from whence our help comes. We know, Lord, that our help comes from You, and we thank You for being a shade at [our] right hand. Lord, Your Word continues to be a shield in battle, and Your Word sets us high in the tower and fortress of Your power and love. Thank You for delivering us from where we were to where we stand today, surrendered by Your anointing and daily protection.

Oh Lord, our God, thank You that we can claim You as ours. Whatever we need in our battles, God supplies. We bless You, God, for Your loving-kindness, and we acknowledge Your love and grace toward Your Chosen Vessels. Lord, we thank You for the relationship that we have in You.

You are our God who is our rock, protector, provider, and peace during storms. Lord, God, [we] come to You on behalf of family, co-workers, and leaders. We have set our hearts toward You and desire to seek after You and declare that You are our God. Father God help us all to see how much You love us, so we can have confidence to declare that You are our God. We honor You for enabling us to cry out to You for help from the depths of our soul. In Your name, Jesus, Your Chosen Vessels say, Amen.

Our God loves us. Read a few other translations of Psalm 144:1-2 as it will bless you to see how Abba is your rock, tower, and deliverer who will allow you to take refuge in Him.

What has God revealed to you as you meditate on the scripture?

Journal

QUESTIONS TO PONDER

God's Support in Battle

1. Have you considered the purpose of why it is so important for you to share your story for such a time as this?
2. What is your passion?
3. Are you willing to persevere and fulfill the plan God has spoken over your life?

What is your prayer today?

Journal

A Legacy of Praise

Prayer Focus: Psalm 145:1-3, NKJV

I will extol You, my God, O King; And I will bless Your name forever and ever. Every day I will bless You, And I will praise Your name forever and ever. Great *is* the Lord and greatly to be praised; And His greatness *is* unsearchable.

Prayer Focus Reflection

Our Lord is allowing us to pour out words of exhortation over one another. As we read Psalm 145, the Lord reminds us that if we call upon Him, He will hear our call. I love that we are a generation of worshippers, and the Lord speaks and answers our prayers. We each have a legacy of praise that we can share with our children, nieces, nephews, aunts, uncles, and various people that the Lord puts in our paths. The word *shall* in Psalm 145:4-6 (NKJV) is defined as *must* (meaning *will have to*) and *can* (meaning *will be able to*.) We have been given the authority to teach someone else of God's goodness and greatness because we as believers must be a generation that praise God's works and declares His mighty acts in our lives to others.

God speaks during silence, and He hears us the very first time we utter a prayer unto Him. It is so true that God is near to all who call, and His Word is true that He will cover our families and heal them from all sicknesses and diseases. God upholds families, and we can trust that men will have to speak of the might of God's awesome acts and declare His greatness. God will open our hearts and speak clearly to us.

Pray for compassion so that we each take time to show love to those loved ones who have addictions. The Lord is more than able to remove the anger, shame, and self-doubt that a loved one maybe facing. God will show compassion and meet the addict right where they are, because the "Lord is good to all." We declare that those dealing with alcoholism or any other addiction will accept the Lord's tender mercies and His works and begin to praise God for their deliverance.

God will open windows of opportunity in our lives as we become still and know that El Shaddai, the all-sufficient one, is all that we need. Each time we come to God in prayer we are declaring that we are in relationship with Him. When we incline our ear to hear what Abba says, He cultivates our faith because we are committed to being in personal contact with him. The Lord will use our stories to help someone else, and we will pass on the legacy of praise, because we must share God's goodness.

Our daily encounters teach us God's truth, and we learn how to be examples and to creatively share with others that the Lord will fill us and quench our thirsts with His anointing. All He requires is that we trust in Him.

QUESTIONS TO PONDER

A Legacy of Praise

1. Have you considered why it is so important to leave a legacy for such a time as this?
2. What is your passion?
3. Are you willing to persevere and fulfill the plan God has spoken over your life?

What is your prayer today?

Journal

PRAYER THEME

Hallelujah Praises

Prayer Focus: Psalm 146:1-3, NKJV

Praise the LORD! Praise the LORD, O my soul! While I live, I will praise the LORD; I will sing praises to my God while I have my being. Do not put your trust in princes, *Nor* in a son of man, in whom *there* is no help.

Prayer Focus Reflection

It is exciting to reflect and praise God. I am excited about how the Lord is going to bless all who read this prayer focus reflection. The Lord has a work for us to do, and He is asking us to surrender to Him and position ourselves to be His watchmen or watchwomen on the wall. It is important for us to cry out in prayer to God. It is time for us to encircle our families with prayer and a continual praise.

We all have faced many blessings and challenges, and we should praise the Lord for both. Psalms 146:1-2 makes this clear and each of these scriptures begins with the words praise the Lord in English, but the Hebrew translation means to be clear. The Psalmist is teaching us to put our confidence as well as trust in God. No matter what you or your spouse or your child or your grandchild or any relative or workplace may face, Abba is near us. Throughout the Psalms, we are to focus our attention on praising the Lord.

Psalm 146 tells us it is good and pleasant to praise the Lord; the Psalm begins with a vow to praise our God throughout life. We are to trust God in all circumstances and praise the Lord for His goodness. God cares for His people, and He will see us through. Let us exalt Him. Let us magnify Lord for He is worthy to be praised! This Psalm is teaching us to be grateful people who believe with our whole heart that all things work together for our good. Through this Psalm, the Lord our God is teaching us to turn from constant anxiety or a spirit of hurry and discouragement and begin to put our focus on the Lord instead. Throughout Psalm 146, the phrase "Praise the Lord" is mentioned over and over again.

Take some time today and pray a prayer of thanks, let us pray:

Thank You, Abba Father, for everything. Thank You for food, clothing, and shelter; thank You, Lord God, for meeting all our needs above and beyond all that we can ask or think – in the name of Jesus Christ our Lord and Savior.

Jehovah God, we are so thankful for another day, and another opportunity to do Your will today. We are so honored to be Your child; we will forever praise You while we have our being because You are worthy to be praised. Thank You, Abba Father, for the joy, laughter, good health, and prosperity in all aspects of our lives. We give You all the glory and honor. In Jesus Christ's name we pray, Amen.

QUESTIONS TO PONDER

Hallelujah Praises

1. Have you considered whether you will purpose yourself to be a watchperson for God?

2. How has your passion for praise and worship helped you during tests and trials?

3. Are you willing to persevere as well as praise the Lord no matter what?

What is your prayer today?

Journal

PRAYER THEME

The Healer Rebuilds the Brokenhearted

Prayer Focus: Psalm 147:1-3, NKJV

Praise the LORD! For *it is* good to sing praises to our God; For *it is* pleasant, *and* praise is beautiful. The LORD builds up Jerusalem; He gathers together the outcasts of Israel. He heals the brokenhearted and binds up their wounds.

Prayer Focus Reflection

This is the Lord's Day, and our aim is to rejoice and be glad as a vessel of God. We are in a cycle of change. As you know, it takes twenty-one days to change a habit. I believe we are committed to change old habits, and I am convinced that we each will have a deeper thirst for God's Word as a result. God's Word quenches those who are thirsty. Even when you are feeling down and uncertain, know that God's Word does not return void. God promises restoration! Restoration means to bring something back to its former position or condition.

As we reflect on the last four chapters in Psalms, we are reminded to praise our God. Each one who has this book in hand has chosen a prayer warrior stance as a Chosen Vessel gap filler, Christ-following Intercessor, who is committed to praying for others.

Psalm 147:1-3 shows us the benefits of having a pattern of praise and His ability to heal those that are brokenhearted. Reflect on the following words during your prayer time: *pleasant, beautiful, build* and *heals*. Take a few minutes to read and reflect on Psalm 147; see what God says to you about restoration.

Psalm 147 offered a model through David's prayer life. This modeled prayer brought restoration into David's life. Just as David was restored by being a man of prayer and praise, we too, can experience God's care, mercy, love, and joy, and can sing a song of praise in unison. Our song could be, "Lord, every day no matter what, we will commit to pray and praise your holy name." Christ's love grants us an opportunity to walk this path of restoration to take us back to our proper place as joint heirs who are connected to Abba, Father.

In closing, prayer brings restoration to all if we obey. We should take time daily to pray that through our experiences, our prayers will generate a movement of souls being saved, relationships with God being restored, and others experiencing the beautiful hope that God builds on His righteousness. Let us continue to pray. Let us shout, "Hallelujah" and sing praises to our God in advance for the many souls that will be added to his kingdom. Praise God and thank Him for His love and restoration from our brokenness and making us no longer outcasts.

QUESTIONS TO PONDER

The Healer Rebuilds the Brokenhearted

1. Have you considered whether you are ready for restoration, which is God's purpose for your life?
2. How has your passion for restoration in life's circumstances helped you in this season of brokenness in your life?
3. Are you willing to persevere and go beyond your present state of brokenness in your new season of restoration no matter what?

What is your prayer today?

Journal

PRAYER THEME

Creation Can Praise God and So Can We

Prayer Focus: Psalm 148:1-3, NKJV

Praise the LORD! Praise the LORD from the heavens; Praise Him in the heights! Praise Him, all His angels; Praise Him, all His hosts! Praise Him, sun, and moon; Praise Him, all you stars of light!

Prayer Focus Reflection

Use prayer to fight for your family. Recognize that prayer is an offensive weapon. It will help us defeat the blows of the enemy. Our prayers and praise can serve as knockout punches that will bring restoration to our homes, our communities, and our workplaces.

As we offer songs of praise unto God, this will help us to create an atmosphere of praise. Having a song of praise on your lips promotes praise. Also, an effective prayer life promotes a desire to praise God every day. Our spending time with God daily helps us to develop a divine spiritual connection with Abba, Father. Through our relationship with our God, we know that He can help us on this journey of life. God will bring restoration to our relationships, but it requires that we trust Him no matter what. Your relationships matter to God. Therefore, wherever we are in this journey of life, God will restore our relationships. We have been positioned for such a time as this to be God's Chosen Vessel. He loves us so much that He daily beckons us to fellowship with Him. Our quiet time ushers us into a deeper relationship with the Lord. Our prayers today and in the days to come are to allow the presence of God to stimulate our minds and create a song unto God. Sing a song unto God thanking Him for His grace and mercy unto us.

When you read the word creation, what comes to your mind? Creation includes the elements like wind, sun, stars, trees, rain as well as the four seasons. God's purpose for wind is to offer a breeze during a hot day. The sun's purpose is to bring warmth to the earth. When thinking of the creation, one thinks of the stars God created to shine. God provides food for the animals from the plants that flourish during each of the four seasons. Rain replenishes the earth. Rain restores the land, the streams, the leaves, the grass, and God's creation. Rain generates growth and stimulates the earth. Some of us are dry and desolate, but God can bring rain in your life to bring restoration to you and your situations. Remember, God's Word has the power to bring healing.

In closing, our prayers today will bring healing and restoration to every corner of our heart, mind, and soul. As we reflect on creation, remember that God's love will bring restoration in our lives. Our commitment to the Creator will help to create a deeper relationship with the Lord. So, take time during the rest of this week to praise the Lord. Continue to pray God's Word, because it will heal, restore, nourish, and reveal some remarkable things to you.

Shout praises to God because He has the power to minister to the brokenhearted. He can deliver our wayward children, husbands, and family members. God has given us direct access to Him morning, noon, and night. We have a direct line to His throne, and we can experience fullness of joy. Let us continue to pray for the thousands upon thousands of souls that will be added to God's kingdom. Continue to give thanks and pray in the name of the Lord, our Savior, Jesus Christ every day.

QUESTIONS TO PONDER

Creation Can Praise God and So Can We

1. Have you considered how understanding the purpose to pray and praise God matters to our relationships, especially during times you need to fight for your family?
2. What are your passions in pursuing God as your Redeem who renovates and allows you to sing unto Him a new song?
3. Are you willing to persevere and go the distance no matter what tries to separate you from your purpose and God-ordained passions?

What is your prayer today?

Journal

PRAYER THEME

Sing Unto the Lord a New Song

Prayer Focus: Psalm 149:1-3, NKJV

Praise the LORD! Sing to the LORD a new song, *And* His praise in the assembly of saints. Let Israel rejoice in their Maker; Let the children of Zion be joyful in their King. Let them praise His name with the dance; Let them sing praises Him with the timbrel and harp.

Prayer Focus Reflection

We each have committed to make some significant changes, and the Lord has given us some principles that we can place in our premarital and marital toolbox. The use of offensive weapons like prayer and praise helps us to defeat the blows of the enemy.

Chosen Vessels, purpose-driven prayers and continual praise combined make a knockout punch. These knockout punches have the word *restoration* written on each hand. Since God is the way, the truth, and the life, then we can have joy and embrace the path He has outlined for us.

Imagine, if you will, a block of clay in the hands of a potter. The potter reshapes the clay into many forms to remove the air bubbles. As God's Chosen Vessels, sometimes we must be placed on the potter's wheel or be remade. As we all know, when God restores, He puts things back in their former position or condition. He reconditions, which includes our homes being placed in the proper place and condition, and our communities and workplaces being restored to their former position or condition. Pastor John K. Jenkins, Sr., my pastor, shared a great phrase in one of his sermons: "Marriage is a character developer." As I wrote down those words, I thought about a book I read entitled, *Sacred Marriage* where the author said, "Marriage is not about happiness; it is about holiness." God spoke to me, and I wrote, *God is a character shaper. Allow Him to mold and make me.*

This leads to today's thought from Psalm 149:1-4 (NLT). The Psalmist says to the reader,

> "Sing to the Lord a new song. Sing his praises in the assembly of the faithful. O Israel, rejoice in your Maker. O people of Jerusalem exult in your King. Praise Him with dancing, accompanied by tambourine and harp. For the Lord delights in His people, He crowns the humble with salvation."

For some time now, corporate prayer has been a lifeline for some as we have made a daily commitment to pray for our spouses, families, and communities. There is a blessing in being consistent and continually praising God, despite what comes into our midst. In Psalm 149:2, we see the urgency of the Psalmist regarding the importance of rejoicing in our Maker, our Creator. God takes joy in our praising Him for His salvation and judgment. May we always have a song of praise on our lips and in our hearts.

As we commit to spend time with the Lord, we are positioning ourselves into a rhythm of prayer. This self-sanctioned quiet time helps us to develop spiritual discernment, so we can hear God's voice and silence the enemy's voice with God's praise on our lips.

Our spending time with God daily helps us to develop a divine spiritual connection with Abba Father. Through our relationship with our God, we know that He can help us on this journey of life. As you surrender your mind, your fears, and your pain, God our Maker has purposed a way of truth and life. God's sovereignty speaks restoration to all relationships when we submit to Him.

Totally surrendering situations to God has positive effects. Even when things look bleak and rather dreary, we can have confidence that God who is powerful can turn things completely around. What we need to do is trust Him, then He will see us through. The truth of the matter is that God can do exceedingly and abundantly above all that we can even think or ask (Ephesians 3:20).

Worship is a continual process, and when we are in a proper stance of worship, then we can serve and minister to others—married, unmarried, young, and old. It is important for us to share our testimony, our story with someone else. Scripture says when two or three come together, God is in the midst; there is power in corporate prayer. When we pray for relationships and take the matter to God, change happens (Matthew 18:20). An unknown author once said,

"Life is fragile, handle with prayer."

Therefore, at whatever state you are in on this journey of life, if you feel your relationships are happy, crappy, or snappy, the Lord will place us in the proper place. You have been positioned for such a time as this to be God's Chosen Vessel. He loves us so much that He daily beckons us to fellowship with Him. Your quiet time ushers you into a deeper relationship with the Lord and your praying and praising God builds your faith.

The Lord God our Maker desires us to walk in truth and in love. Our Maker desires us to worship Him fervently, and we can worship Him in our own interpretive dance and sing a new song. We are worshiping God every time we pray God's Word, read God's Word, and offer words of exhortation to another and share that they too can make it. When we share the gospel and let all know that God will see them through, when we sing hymns and songs of praise, we are in a posture of worshiping our Maker. Our purpose, Chosen Vessels, is to delight ourselves in the Lord, for when we do this, we bring Him immense joy.

In closing, our prayers today will bring boundless joy to our Maker. Through our singing, we bring a praise offering unto our God. Through our praises, prayers, and songs, we are focusing our worship on God and not in entertaining Him but in exalting Him for who He is. He is our healer. He is our way Maker. He is our keeper. He is our truth. He is love, and He is more than able to restore every fissure in our hearts, minds, and souls.

As you reflect on our Maker, remember that God's love brings hope and purpose. Our commitment to the Maker will help us to praise Him with our very being. Prayer and praise usher us into worship. The Lord gave us direct access to Him when He went to Calvary. We have a direct pathway to God's mighty throne of grace. Through our praises, we can be confident that the Maker, who loves us, knows us, and completes us, will help us to experience His fullness of joy. We give thanks and seal this encouraging word in the name of the Lord, our Savior, Jesus Christ, Amen.

QUESTIONS TO PONDER

Sing Unto the Lord a New Song

1. Would you agree that our purpose is to delight ourselves in the Lord?

2. Do passions help us to have a stronger commitment to our Maker?

3. Are you willing to persevere and go the distance no matter what path is set before you?

What is your prayer today?

Journal

PRAYER THEME

The Beauty of High Praise

Prayer Focus: Psalm 150:1-3, NKJV

Praise the LORD! Praise God in His sanctuary; Praise Him in His mighty firmament! Praise Him for His mighty acts; Praise Him according to His excellent greatness! Praise Him with the sound of the trumpet; Praise Him with the lute and harp!

Prayer Focus Reflection

When you hear the word beauty, what comes to your mind? I think of *loveliness, graceful,* and *belle. Merriam Webster Dictionary* defines beauty as *the quality of being physically attractive or the qualities in a person or a thing that gives pleasure to the senses or the mind.* If we apply *Merriam Webster Dictionary* definition, using the latter portion of the definition, we could say that Chosen Vessels who praise (exhort, magnify, and reverence) God have qualities that give pleasure to the senses or the mind.

This leads to our prayer focus for today, the beauty of having a high praise for God. Psalm 150:5-6 tells us,

> Praise Him with loud clashing cymbals; Praise Him with clashing cymbals! Let everything that has breath praise the Lord! Praise the LORD!

The Psalmist has asked us here to worship the Lord. He highlights to us that when we focus on praising the Lord, when we express high praises unto God's mighty works and greatness, then we can experience the beauty of God's love toward us as we worship Him in spirit and in truth. Each day, we are given an opportunity to have a covenant relationship that seals us unto the day of redemption. The Lord loves it when we gather and worship Him. We know because we find God's Word to be delightful, beautiful, fruitful, and blissful.

The word *praise*, found in Psalm 150, is used thirteen times in that chapter alone; ten of those times, the Lord gives us specific instruction about how we are to praise Him. In Psalm 150:1-2, we are commanded to focus on God, we see that we can worship God from any geographic location because the Lord fills the heaven and the earth, and we see that the chosen people of God are to praise God's mighty acts. God's mighty acts reveal His character, which include His holiness, love, wisdom, power, and grace, to name just a few.

Finally, we see in Psalm 150:3-6, that our voices serve as a melody of praise in unison with the musical instruments that offer praise unto God. Psalm 150:6 is the doxology or ending word to us in the Book of Psalms, and the Lord declares to us the following:

> "Let everything that has breath praise the Lord."

Remember, true worship is to take the very breath given by God and praise Him daily and above all. God has called every living thing that has breath to praise the Lord with music, singing, and dancing.
In addition, He has called us to be wise Chosen Vessels, and He has given us His Word to direct our lives as He gives us the air we breathe.

QUESTIONS TO PONDER

The Beauty of High Praise

1. Have you considered the purpose in offering God a beautiful, high praise?
2. Are you a passionate worshipper?
3. Are you willing to persevere and go the distance no matter what?

What is your prayer today?

Journal

Praying and Journaling
Proverbs

PRAYER THEME

Wisdom in Listening

Prayer Focus: Proverbs 1:1-3, NKJV

The proverbs of Solomon the son of David, king of Israel: To know wisdom and instruction, To perceive the words of understanding, To receive instruction of wisdom, justice, judgement, and equity.

Prayer Focus Reflection

He lives…our God lives! Our Scripture today comes from Proverbs 1. The Proverbs have some prominent themes such as the fear of the Lord, wisdom, righteousness, purity, justice, wealth…and the value of a godly wife. Each Proverb allows us to reflect, pause, and think about our life's journey. Proverbs serve as "spiritual vitamins" that build us up and causes our thinking to change. Wisdom strengthens our hearts, and wisdom grants us a passion to honor the Lord of our life. The wise nuggets of Proverbs serve as prescription for life and so many lessons, like the ones below:

† Fearing the Lord (Proverbs 1:7)

† Folly of following wicked people (Proverbs 1:8)

† Fringe benefits of getting wisdom (Proverbs 1:20)

† Fantastic value one gains from listening when wisdom cries out (Proverbs 1:33)

Therefore, Chosen Vessels, the Lord is telling us to fear Him and not wicked people, because we can find value in answering Wisdom's call. Read Proverbs 1:2, 5, 7, 8, 20, and 33, then let us pray a corporate prayer of wisdom together:

Dear Lord, Your Chosen Vessels bless You for Your Word. Each time we dwell in Your secret place, You give us a word. You give us hope. You give us wisdom. You give us peace that surpasses our understanding. Father, we thank You for holding us close to You and enabling us to learn of Your wisdom.

Lord, we call unto You and thank You for thoughtfulness. Father God, You freely give [us] the discipline of wise thoughtfulness to serve others in love, joy, and peace. Holy Spirit [teach us] how to gather, reflect, journal, revisit, and act on good health habits and financial decisions. Lord, we thank You for Your resurrection power that is in us. Your resurrection power helps us to think on whatever is true, honest, just, pure, lovely in everyday life. Our thoughtfulness is because of You, Jesus. Thank You, Lord Jesus, for Your thoughtfulness toward us!

Oh Lord, [we] know what it is like to be a fool, yet, You still loves [us] and draw [us] to You and pour Your wisdom upon [us] and fill [us] with it to keep [us] in Your way. Lord, we have all that [we] need in [us] because [we] are complete in You. This includes Your wisdom to lead, instruct, and give us life. [We] thank You God for [Your] wisdom crying out to [us] because Wisdom wants to increase in [us], as [we] hear [Wisdom's call].

Father, we thank You for wisdom because it teaches us to live a godly life, and Your Word directs us and gives us an understanding that it not our way but Your way. Lord, help us to listen and give us instruction and wisdom for our children and youth in general. Help our children to speak boldly and open their hearts to You. Lord, as we hearken unto You, we thank You for teaching us to listen to You so that we may live in safety. Your instruction serves as a safety net, and we can dwell in You by taking heed to Your Word. Father, we ask You to take away all fear because there is power and safety in You. We close this prayer, Lord, by honoring You for enabling us to hear Wisdom's instruction for today and in the days to come. In Your name, Jesus, Your Chosen Vessels say, Amen.

What has God revealed to you as you meditate on the scripture?

Journal

QUESTIONS TO PONDER

Wisdom in Listening

1. What value can you gain from listening when wisdom cries out?
2. Are you willing to apply wisdom as a spiritual vitamin to help you in life?
3. Are there any fringe benefits of applying wisdom in your life journey?

What is your prayer today?

Journal

PRAYER THEME

Consider My Words

Prayer Focus: Proverbs 2:1-3, NKJV

My son, if you receive my words, And treasure my commands within you, So that you incline your ear to wisdom, *And* apply your heart to understanding; Yes, if you cry out for discernment, *And* lift up your voice for understanding.

Prayer Focus Reflection

As you arise today, ask God to consider your words. Ask Abba to guide you throughout the day. You know God honors Vessels who carry His Word in their hearts. As you ponder on today's Scripture, select a few words, and cover your family and your situation. God's Word, love, and grace change not. Rise early and spend time seeking God. Be His Chosen Vessel who allows God to fill you as His container of love, grace, and mercy to influence all those you meet.

QUESTIONS TO PONDER

Consider My Words

1. What were the words that spoke to you during your meditation?
2. Where do your passions lie as His chosen container of love, grace, and mercy?
3. Are you willing to persevere no matter what to influence all those you meet?

What is your prayer today?

Journal

PRAYER THEME

God's Desire Toward Me

Prayer Focus: Proverbs 3:1-3, NKJV

My son do not forget my law, But let your heart keep my commands; For length of days and long life And peace they will add to you. Let not mercy and truth forsake you; Bind them around your neck, Write them on the tablet of your heart.

Prayer Focus Reflection

God asks us to not forget His law given to all who are part of His family. His law sets in motion directives for our lives. A law is a directive. A directive guides us along the way as instructed by God. His way grants us peace…a peace that can lengthen our days because we hinge our way of thinking and behaving upon it, as God ordains for us to do. His way gives us a peace that surpasses our understanding, and we can be certain that His way is always right.

As His children, we are connected to His mercy (which includes His goodness faithfulness, and kindness) as well as His truth (which is His sureness, reliability, and divine instruction, and doctrine). Mercy and truth help us to have an intimate relationship with Abba, Father. Through this intimate relationship, we experience His love toward us…a love that supports us and guides us toward His amazing grace. God's love instills hope when we sometimes feel despair. God is our Father, who art in heaven, and a father's love is continual and never fades away. Abba's love is a binding agent that keeps us connected to our Lord, just like the neck connects the head to the body and supports it. Without the neck, the head cannot exist on its own, nor can the body exist without the head and neck connected. If the neck is severed from the body, the body dies. The love of God the Father seeks to comfort His children and supply all their needs. He is our way maker, our protector, and the guardian of our hearts. Isn't it awesome to know that our Lord, Savior, and God is always with us and will never leave us alone?

The law and the commands of the Father prepare us for everything that may try to distract us. His principles and instructions help us navigate through this journey of life. His Word reminds us to trust Him, and He will direct our paths. Therefore, the Lord reminds us in this passage of Scripture, Proverbs 3:1-3 that the principles (the law and His instructions) are essential to our survival. We cannot do anything without the Lord. When you place God's law, which are His instructions, principles, and commands, around your neck, it binds us to God so that the tempter cannot easily sway us. God's loving instructions and principles should be written, engraved, recorded, decreed, and penned as a covenant within the hearts, intellect, soul, and thinking of His daughters and sons. This covenant promise, or declaration, will serve as a tracker that when we go off the mark; our thinking and intellect will remind us to get back on track and follow the instructions God gave us.

QUESTIONS TO PONDER

God's Desire Towards Me

1. Have you considered penning God's purpose for your life as a witness for Him?
2. Once you pen your passions, how do you plan to share your witness with others?
3. Are you willing to persevere and go the distance no matter what in sharing the wisdom God has given to you?

What is your prayer today?

Journal

PRAYER THEME

Penning Rekindled Passions

Prayer Focus: Proverbs 4:1-3, NKJV

Hear, *my* children, the instruction of a father, And give attention to know understanding; For I give you good doctrine: Do not forsake my law. When I was my father's son, Tender and the only one in the sight of my mother.

Prayer Focus Reflection

From today's prayer theme, did God show Himself to you as you prayed? Do you have a better understanding of His plan for you? Have you rekindled your passion? Are you assured in your purpose?

As you journey in this walk of wisdom, it is important to take time to reflect on how the Lord desires you to receive His Word. Think about how He has beckoned you to treasure His commands. Incline your ear each day to His wisdom and plan for your life. As you apply His precepts, you will hear and get His understanding. By crying out for His spiritual discernment, He will let you know whether your plan is or is not His way. His answer will lift you up, and you should lift your voice with a shout of praise. Praising Him will give you understanding. Seek the wisdom of God, and He will reveal His hidden treasure within you. Continue to journal and be God's pen, with a passion that aims to fulfill your purpose. Understand that your suffering brings wisdom and hope.

Your suffering for His sake has a purpose. God is preparing you and granting you the desires of your heart (no more suffering in bitterness) to receive more knowledge in Him. God will honor your desire and give you more understanding. God will give you a clearer focus on what He is saying because He is stirring up His gift inside of you. God says that you His selected, picked, *Chosen Vessel* serve as His pen, and through this experience of suffering, stretching, and sacrificing for His name's sake, you are stronger in His Word.

As you begin to honor, reverence, and respect those who have rule over you, those to whom you are to yield and submit, you begin to understand the power of trusting God. Yes, He hears us, and He knows our intimate thoughts. Chosen Vessels, place your trust in God.

Do you hear the Lord, He's saying right now that we are "to place" our trust in Him, which means, "position, to get in your spot, to step as He orders." Therefore, Chosen Vessels, remember God has a plan, you have His passion, and you have a purpose. Trust, honor, and obey Him, because Proverbs 4:7 (New International Version) says,

> The beginning of wisdom is this: Get wisdom. Though it cost all you have, get understanding.

In addition, wisdom brings understanding to your home, your situation, your circumstances. Proverbs 2:5-7 (New Kings James Version) tells us,

> Then you will understand the fear of the Lord And find the knowledge of God. For the Lord gives wisdom; From His mouth come knowledge and understanding: He stores up sound wisdom for the upright; He is a shield to those who walk uprightly.

Be blessed, Chosen Vessels, and "turn your ear to wisdom and apply your heart to understanding."

QUESTIONS TO PONDER

Penning Rekindled Passions

1. Have you considered penning God's purpose for your life?
2. Once you pen your passions, how do you plan to share with others how obtaining God's wisdom brings understanding?
3. Are you willing to persevere and go the distance no matter what in sharing sound wisdom?

What is your prayer today?

Journal

PRAYER THEME

Wisdom Takes A Quality Stand

Prayer Focus: Proverbs 8:1-3, NKJV

Does not wisdom cry out, And understanding lift up her voice? She takes her stand on the top of the high hill, Beside the way where the paths meet. She cries out by the gates, at the entry of the city, At the entrance of the doors.

Prayer Focus Reflection

Our Scripture today comes from Chapter 8 in the Book of Proverbs, which gives each Chosen Vessel some biblical nuggets of wisdom in brief sayings on God's perspective for our lives.

The Excellence of Wisdom – NKJV

Excellence in wisdom can lead to favor, which we should all seek. Proverbs 8:26 says, "While as yet He had not made the earth or the fields, or the primal dust of the world." This passage of Scripture taught me that wisdom was at the beginning with God. Our Lord is wisdom, and we are to pattern our lives on God's wisdom instead of human knowledge. We can reach a deeper understanding of the things of God and receive greater revelation and discernment by asking God for wisdom.

Wisdom Call – New International Version

Wisdom's call speaks of an inward knowing. This inward calling is unique and available to us. Our God designs us to receive, and He gives us wisdom for each season of life. If we are new moms, God gives us wisdom to be a mom. If we are grandmothers, God gives us wisdom to be a grandmother. If we are in a season of separation, God gives us wisdom to deal with the circumstances we face. God is generous, and He allows us to choose whether or not to walk in wisdom.

In Praise of Wisdom – Contemporary English Version

Praising wisdom allows us to reach out, praise God, and call out unto Him. When we ask for wisdom and follow God, this enables us to be led by Him. Being led by God's direction helps us to have great understanding as we seek Him.

The Blessing of Wisdom – English Standard Version

The blessing of wisdom teaches us to read and listen to God so we each can walk in a blessed life. Having a walk that is wrapped in wisdom enables us to have peace and joy. Prayer is our lifeline when we pray in God's perfect will. Praying God's Word as found in Proverbs 8 will help us want for nothing and walk in joy because of our connection to Abba Father.

Let us pray to be wise vessels:

Father, Your Chosen Vessels stand on Your Word. We are opening our mouth to speak truth and to speak life over any dead situation(s). Lord, we stand on Proverbs 8:7, which says, "For my mouth will speak truth; Wickedness is an abomination to my lips." Help us all to be truth tellers who speak in love, joy, and peace.

Lord, we want to walk in holy discretion and not arrogance. Help us, Lord, to speak and walk this life in sound judgment. We, Lord, desire to seek You in every aspect of our lives. Thank You, Lord, for giving us an opportunity to seek You first and follow Your direction so that our lives can be blessed.

God, help us to be right. Your wisdom was with the Lord before the earth was even formed. Lord, we want You to be first in our lives and ask that You help us to live a life of holiness and righteousness. Birth in us, dear Lord, a passion to reach all who fall within the boundaries You have called us to walk. This is our prayer, dear Jesus.

Abba, we delight in You. We rejoice in being able to call unto Your name. We bless You that You love us so much that You gave us Your Word and instruction to live this holy life. You are the only wise God. Thank You, dear Lord, for speaking to us today. We heard Your word: "Listen to me because I am love and I have given you life; listen and be obedient."

Finally, Lord, we are so grateful that in You we find and receive protection and wisdom because of our relationship and connection to You! We seal these prayers and offer words of encouragement over the Chosen Vessel family members, the minds of our youth, and our daily Christian walk. We bless You, dear Lord, for the opportunity to gain experience that, before the world was formed, wisdom was there! We are grateful for Proverbs 8:35 (NIV) "For those who find me (Wisdom) find life and receive favor from the Lord."

Lord, we honor You today for enabling us to hear Wisdom's instruction for today and the days to come. Amen.

QUESTIONS TO PONDER

Wisdom Takes a Quality Stand

1. Have you considered how you will stand on God's Word for your life today?
2. How do you plan to make the Lord first in your life today?
3. Are you willing to speak truth and life to allow peace and joy to manifest in your life?

What is your prayer today?

Journal

PRAYER THEME

How Wisdom Instructs Us

Prayer Focus: Proverbs 9:1-3, NKJV

Wisdom has built her house, She has hewn out seven pillars; She has slaughtered her meat, She has mixed her wine, She has also furnished her table. She has sent out her maidens, She cries out from the highest places of the city.

Prayer Focus Reflection

There is so much power when we pray and call upon the Lord's name, speak about His Word, and apply the lesson of wisdom to our daily lives. Today, I reflected on my mother's surgery when I had to stand on what the Lord has been teaching us, to trust God in every situation. I constantly reminded myself to not lean to my own understanding but in all my ways to acknowledge God so that He could direct my path. I had to stand on the wisdom that my mother has graciously taught me through the years as I found myself a little uncomfortable that her surgery was no longer an outpatient, but now an inpatient. However, when I read and talked about the Word, I began to hear God's comfort found in Proverbs 9:10-11 (NKJV), which says,

> Fear of the Lord is the beginning of wisdom. Knowledge of the Holy One results in understanding. Wisdom will multiply your days and add years to your life.

This journey through Proverbs offers great wisdom, and it teaches godly principles that will prepare us to sup with our Lord daily. I really like how this Proverb starts. Solomon lets us know that, "Wisdom has built her spacious house with seven pillars. She has prepared a great banquet, mixed with wines, and set the table." These two passages of Scripture really speak that wisdom can oversee any situation in life, and that we can each receive by following and embracing wisdom and releasing foolishness.

Throughout today's reflection, wisdom offers essential instructions for us to live each day. Wisdom helps us to mingle with the right people instead of foolish people. Wisdom allows us to discern simplemindedness (foolishness). Through wisdom, we can receive a "no" answer but understand God's wisdom offers protection in walking in the unknown places as the Lord orders our steps. We learn from abiding by the Scripture that wisdom can give instruction in raising children, in understanding God's Word, and in keeping a household, and fulfilling our purpose on a job. In addition, we learn that when wisdom is applied to our everyday lives and when we obey, we receive a good reward.

As Proverbs, 9:9 says, "Teach the wise, and they will be wiser. Teach the righteous, and they will learn more." Therefore, Chosen Vessels, each day when we come together to study God's Word, each day that we surrender unto Him, each day we are becoming wiser, each day we are getting stronger, and each day we are getting better. Remember, God has a plan, you have His passion and a purpose. Come and eat from God's table and receive wisdom. Proverbs 9:4-6 commands us,

> Whoever is simple, let him turn in here! As for him who lacks understanding, she says to him, Come, eat of my bread, And drink of the wine I have mixed. Forsake foolishness and

> live And go in the way of understanding. (NKJV)
> If you are simple, then come here! She says this to the unwise people. Come, and eat my food! Drink the wine that I have poured! Leave your simple ways and live wisely! (ESV)

Solomon added an explanation to his son about wisdom. He desired to help his son see how choices that were opposite of wisdom caused people to be foolish and how this could influence the nation from Solomon's perspective. Finally, Proverbs 9:4-6 explains to us as believers that we must make wise choices, and if we choose to be around "simple" people, know that our role and responsibility is to teach the unwise about God and show them the right way as we lead them to Him. Wisdom helps and invites all kinds of people to her home because as Proverbs 9:1 says, "Wisdom built her house, She has hewn out her seven pillars." The way of wisdom can accommodate all who come to eat from the table: the poor (needy), the blind, and the lame. All people can learn from wisdom to trust God and live wisely. Chosen Vessels, let us hold on to Proverbs 9:9, which says,

> Give instruction to a wise man, and he will be still wiser;
> Teach a just man, and he will increase in learning. (NKJV)

Finally, let us daily reflect on God's Word and become wise Chosen Vessels who come to know God more and more.

Chosen Vessels, each day you are getting wiser and stronger by reading, praying, and studying God's Word! Let us keep moving forward in our quest to know God more intimately! Take time today to listen to the voice of God.

QUESTIONS TO PONDER

How Wisdom Instructs Us

1. Have you considered whether you really trust God for the purpose He has for your life?
2. How have your passions leveled during this season of life?
3. Are you willing to persevere and go the distance no matter what and follow the instructions of the Lord?

What is your prayer today?

Journal

PRAYER THEME

Following Instructions Makes Us Wiser

Prayer Focus: Proverbs 9:9-12, NKJV

Give *instruction* to a wise *man*, and he will be still wiser. Teach a just *man*, and he will increase in learning. The fear of the LORD *is* the beginning of wisdom, And the knowledge of the Holy One *is* understanding. For by me your days will be multiplied, And years of life will be added to you. If you are wise, you are wise for yourself, And *if* you scoff, you will bear *it* alone.

Prayer Focus Reflection

Have you ever been so excited about something that you could not wait to share the blessing with another? Well, Chosen Vessels, I felt a little deflated. I prepared a special meal for my family that I'd never cooked before. I followed the instructions in the recipe up to the final ingredient before adding the recipe's sauce. I made one substitution to the recipe because I thought I could make a minor change to align with the tastebuds of my family. I share this because I was so excited about making the new recipe, but once I did not follow the instructions, the recipe became my own creation. We sometimes think we know what is best, and we change the instructions that God gives us. This is not right. Have you ever been in a similar situation and changed things according to your own instructions?

Today's Scripture Proverbs 9:9-12 served as my counselor and teacher for today. It teaches us that the wise accepts and welcomes rebuke because they understand they can learn from it and become even wiser. I experienced a spiritual lesson today on good and evil. I could have had an attitude, become a scoffer, and brought havoc into our house.

Instead, I decided that I wanted to grow in God's grace, and I wanted to please God and show honor and respect and make a wise choice. I wanted to follow the instructions God gives so that I could be all that God calls for me to be. These verses offer each of us a personal account of wisdom and confirms that God's Word and acts are dynamic. The wisdom of God gives us life and serves as a foreshadowing of God's divine wisdom for our lives. Proverbs 9:9-12 informs us that wisdom points us in God's ordained direction for our lives. His way shows us God's divine character and allows us to have a greater revelation of who He is, as found in Exodus 3:14:

> And God said to Moses, "I AM WHO I AM." And He said, "Thus you shall say to the children of Israel, 'I AM has sent me to you.'"

As Proverbs 9:9 says, "Give instruction to a wise man, and he will be still wiser." Chosen Vessels, I AM WHO I AM can help us in every aspect of our lives. His indwelling presence is our eternal Guide, Counselor, Helper, Redeemer, Restorer, and Repairer of the Breach. The Great I AM biblical instruction will teach those who desire to learn, and when we reverence God, this is the beginning of wisdom. I must confess that I said to myself, *Lord, You took the preparation of a meal and made me wise.* I had to thank God right then for being a multiplier in my life. My prayer this day was, "Lord, help me to become wiser and stronger in this daily walk."

Therefore, Chosen Vessels, seek wisdom and get understanding in every situation that is destined for you for such a time as this because, if you ask for wisdom, you will get it directly from the Great I AM.

Let us pray and ask God for wisdom:

Lord God Almighty, our blessed Savior and keeper, we come to You today and beseech You as Your blood-bought children and ask for wisdom. Abba, You have given us access, and Your Word says to ask, and it shall be given, and seek and we shall find. Lord God Almighty, we ask You to grant us wisdom. We desire to learn more of Your grace.

Help us to be good stewards over our families. Help us not to walk in and lean to our own way of doing things. Help us to follow Your divine instructions, line upon line. Dear Lord, help us to reflect on Your sovereignty as our great I AM. Keep us, Lord, and forgive us for any decisions we have made or tried to make without seeking You first. We thank You, Lord, for wisdom, grace, and favor. We look to You as our wise counsellor. It is in Your name, Jesus, we pray, Amen.

What has God revealed to you as you meditate on the scripture?

____

____

____

____

____

____

____

____

____

________________________________ *Journal*

QUESTIONS TO PONDER

Following Instructions Makes Us Wiser

1. Have you considered the value of speaking wisdom to fulfill God's purpose for your life?
2. Once you open your mouth and share your passions, how will you figure out when it is wise to share and when it is wise to be silent?
3. Are you willing to persevere and go the distance no matter what in sharing the wisdom God has given you?

What is your prayer today?

Journal

PRAYER THEME

Wisdom Yields Righteous Blessings

Prayer Focus: Proverbs 10:6-10, NKJV

Blessings *are* on the head of righteous, But violence covers the mouth of the wicked. The memory of the righteous *is* blessed. But the name of the wicked will rot. The wise in heart will receive commands, but a prating fool will fall.

Prayer Focus Reflection

Righteous and *righteousness* are words found in Proverbs 10 on multiple occasions. We find the same word in James 5:16, which says,

> Confess your trespasses to one another, and pray for one another, that you may be healed. The effective, fervent prayer of a righteous man avails much.

However, we tend to forget what the word *avails* means. According to the *Merriam Webster Dictionary*, it means *to produce or result in as a benefit or advantage: gain.* As righteous (upright) Chosen Vessels, our conduct should conform to God's standards and moral character, which will help us to gain or produce a right relationship with the Lord. The Lord desires that we be righteous Chosen Vessels who obey His commandments. Coming together in prayer offers healing to our broken situations because there is power in prayer.

Wisdom offers us a path that will yield restoration and joy in our lives. Therefore, Chosen Vessels, accept your healing by allowing the righteousness of God to direct your path so you can experience His blessings of joy, restoration, and peace. Obey God and let go. Do not pick up what you surrendered; trust God, because He is in control. Remember, He is the master artisan or crafter of our lives.

Let us offer a prayer unto the master artisan:

Lord God Almighty, Creator of the Universe, we, Your fervent prayer warriors, are yielding our thoughts to You. We ask You, Abba, to help us assume a posture that offers You praise and adoration. We aim to be wise in heart and not foolish; we desire to be in the posture to receive a crown of blessings for Your righteousness's sake. Keep us, Lord, and help us to align ourselves with Your divine Word. In Your name, Jesus, we pray, Amen.

What has God revealed to you as you meditate on the scripture?

____

____

____

____

____

____

____

____

____

______________________________ *Journal*

QUESTIONS TO PONDER

Wisdom Yields Righteous Blessings

1. Have you considered how wisdom yields righteous blessings?
2. Do you think that your applying wisdom will yield restorative joy in your life?
3. Are you willing to persevere and be a fervent prayer warrior who is yielded to receive God's commands?

What is your prayer today?

Journal

PRAYER THEME

The Power of Speaking Wise Words

Prayer Focus: Proverbs 10:19-21, NKJV

In the multitude of words sin is not lacking, But he who restrains his lips *is* wise. The tongue of the righteous *is* choice silver; The heart of the wicked *is worth* little. The lips of the righteous feed many, But fools die for lack of wisdom.

Prayer Focus Reflection

Many times, when we speak, we forget the power of the tongue. Life and death are in the tongue. The Scripture reminds us in Proverbs 10:19-22 that the words we use can either do harm or do good when we apply wisdom.

Have you faced obstacles in your life over the past week? When you consider those obstacles, were they caused by words that came out of your mouth? Well, you are not alone; we have all had to ponder words we have said in our homes, on our jobs, and in our own minds.

God has given us many examples of how to allow wisdom to teach us the value of having and using wise sayings. The Lord gives us an opportunity to command our mornings, put on His armor, and use our offensive weapon of prayer. Chosen Vessels, we must equip ourselves for war.

We need our war clothes, and we need to decree our war cry. We are to gather our children and our kindred and cover them with love and try to do things differently than we have in the past. We are committed to move out of our comfort zones and look for ways to be a blessing in our communities and across the nation.

Prayer is one way to obtain wisdom. Sharing with others by using our mouths to spread the good news about our God serves as another way to walk in wisdom. In addition, being silent when our flesh wants to speak also proves wisdom, because it shows that we know when to speak and when not to speak using the spirit of self-control.

During our quiet time of silence before God, let us seek to know what the Lord wants us to do. Let us begin to ask ourselves whether we are positioning ourselves to be attuned to God's wise ways, so our quality of life will be better. We each know that at times, yes, we will stumble and perhaps even fall, but God has given us wisdom to live by.
Proverbs 10:20-21 tells us,

> The tongue of the righteous is choice silver; The heart of the wicked is worth little. The lips of the righteous feed many, But fools die for lack of wisdom.

This passage of Scripture reminds us of the value of being righteous Chosen Vessels and that the fruit of our lips can feed the multitudes within our communities. Finally, let us keep this thought close to our hearts: Never will there come a time when God will not be there for you. When God says, "Never will I leave you; never will I forsake you" (Hebrews 13:5), He means just that—NEVER [EVER]!

Therefore, Chosen Vessels, put on your war clothes. Don your helmet of salvation, grasp your sword of the spirit, put on your breast plate of righteousness and your shield of faith, gird your loins with truth, shod your feet with peace, and use your offensive weapon of prayer to fight for your marriages, your families, and your communities.

Let us pray and ask God to equip us for battle:

Father, we ask you to equip us to go to battle and pray for our families, our communities, our economy, and our nation. We ask You, Lord, to help us speak wisdom into the atmosphere to bring You glory and honor. In Your name, Jesus, we pray, Amen.

What has God revealed to you as you meditate on the scripture?

Journal

QUESTIONS TO PONDER

The Power of Speaking Wise Words

1. Have you considered how silence could be your best medicine or healing agent?
2. Once you open your mouth and share your passions, how do your words make others feel?
3. Are you willing to allow silence to prove wisdom during times of friction and conflict?

What is your prayer today?

Journal

PRAYER THEME

What Does Love Have to Do with Wise Instructions?

Prayer Focus: Proverbs 12:1-4, NKJV

Whoever loves instruction loves knowledge, But he who hates correction *is* stupid. A good *man* obtains favor from the LORD, But a man of wicked intentions He will condemn. A man is not established by wickedness, But the root of the righteous cannot be moved. An excellent wife *is* the crown of her husband, But she who causes shame *is* like rottenness in his bones.

Prayer Focus Reflection

When one thinks about what love has to do with wise instructions, wisdom echoes in the background. The Lord loves us so much, and it is vital that we trust God and stand on His Word. We are to take hold of God's Word and apply it to every circumstance.

Many of us have family and friends who have been under attack at an alarming rate, and we have faced some challenges ourselves; but we must hold on to God's truth and uncompromising Word that He has spoken to us in His still, small voice and through His abiding Word that is beneficial to all who are standing on His promises and taking Him at His Word.

As you reflect on Proverbs 12:1-4 today, you will see firsthand that love has a lot to do with our existence. It was because of God's love for humanity that He gave His only begotten Son to give us a hope and a future. His love teaches us about His faith, power, grace, and anointing. God's love wavers not. God's love offers life and can quench our thirst. God's love guides and can bring restoration to dead situations.

Proverbs 12:1-4 NLT

> To LEARN, you must want to be taught. To refuse reproof is stupid. The Lord blesses good men and condemns the wicked. Wickedness never brings real success; only the godly have that. A worthy wife is her husband's joy and crown; the other kind corrodes his strength and tears down everything he does.

Proverbs 12:1-3 NKJV

> Whoever loves instruction loves knowledge, But he who hates correction is stupid. A good man obtains favor from the Lord, But a man of wicked intentions He will condemn. A man is not established by wickedness, But the root of the righteous cannot be moved.

God is telling us to have moral character to be all that our God wants and desires us to be. We are worth it. We are virtuous, Chosen Vessels, and we have the power and faith to cause a destiny shift in areas where the Lord has anointed us to be because He has given us His wisdom to be resourceful wives. The world would have you think that you cannot make it or that you are not valuable to God's kingdom. However, this thought is far from the truth, because obedience to God and listening and abiding by His Word makes you wise and full of God's favor. No matter what you are going through, remember that spending time with wise people and studying God's Word enables us to grow in the knowledge of Christ to be His mighty disciples. We are equipped with our offensive weapon of prayer and gifted to serve the people that God has planned for us to serve.

Therefore, Chosen Vessels, seek God, praise God, worship God and #PasstheSalt because when #ChosenVesselsPray, God gets all the glory and the praise. He loves us, so let us offer a prayer asking for His help on our journey:

Father, we seek your grace, knowing that it is sufficient. Help us to seek Your wisdom and apply it in every decision and opportunity that comes before us. In Your name, Jesus, we pray, Amen.

What has God revealed to you as you meditate on the scripture?

Journal

QUESTIONS TO PONDER

What Does Love Have to Do with Wise Instructions?

1. What is God's uncompromising truth that He is speaking over you today?
2. How do you plan to share God's uncompromising truth with others?
3. Are you willing to persevere and go the distance no matter based on the instructions God gave you during your moments of silence today?

What is your prayer today?

Journal

Heeding to Instructions

Prayer Focus: Proverbs 13:1-3, NKJV

A wise son heeds his father's instruction, But a scoffer does not listen to rebuke. A man shall eat well by the fruit of his mouth, But the soul of the unfaithful feeds on violence. He who guards his mouth preserves his life, But he who opens wide his lips shall have destruction.

Prayer Focus Reflection

Throughout today, set out to be His witness. Call God's name on behalf of the sick, be it family members, loved ones from across the United States or friends. Know power is manifested from Chosen Vessels found on their knees. We must increase our understanding and recognize the yielded benefits of pouring out some salt as God's anointed vessels.

Chosen Vessels do not let anyone tell you or make you feel that your prayer life is not necessary. The prayers of the righteous avail much. Our Scripture today, Proverbs 13:1-3, speaks on how wisdom and wise counsel can help family and our friends, as well as every decision for life and ministry. Scripture tells us that youth, children, and we as adults should accept correction from our parents, elders, pastors, and those who have rule over us. Let us really begin to focus on true success, which is working smarter according to the principles that our Lord has outlined for us in His Word to accomplish what God has destined for us.

As we reflect on Proverbs 13:1-25, let us aim to be diligent Chosen Vessels who really understand and can share with others something about the grace of God that is surrounding all of us today and in the days to come. Be blessed, Chosen Vessels, and remember to remain connected to wise counsel and share some salt about how God's grace has kept you, too.

Let us pray:

Father, Your grace is sufficient. Let us continue to remember to hold true to You in every decision and opportunity that comes before us. In Your name, Jesus, we pray, Amen.

What has God revealed to you as you meditate on the scripture?

Journal

QUESTIONS TO PONDER

Heeding to Instructions

1. How has heeding God's instructions benefited you today?
2. How has applying wisdom to life circumstances helped you prevail?
3. Are you willing to guard your mouth and remain connected to wise counsel?

What is your prayer today?

Journal

PRAYER THEME

Wisdom is Like a Life-Giving Fountain

Prayer Focus: Proverbs 13:14-18, NKJV

The law of the wise *is* a fountain of life, To turn *one* away from the snares of death. Good understanding gains favor, But the way of the unfaithful *is* hard. Every prudent *man* acts with knowledge, But a fool lays open *his* folly. A wicked messenger falls into trouble, But a faithful ambassador *brings* health. Poverty and shame *will* come to him who disdains correction, But he who regards a rebuke will be honored.

A Prayer of Reflection

Abba Father, who art in heaven, we, Your Chosen Vessels, come to You today primarily to praise You. Father, we thank You for Your Word. We bless You for setting the Word in motion for us this day. Your Word teaches us how wisdom yields good sense and favor. Whatever man puts for evil, Lord, You can turn it around for our good. Lord, help each wife, husband, daughter, son, sister, brother, cousin, friend, prayer warrior, and anointed vessel to align their words and deeds as wise, respectable vessels.

Help us, Lord, to have good sense in our dealings. Let us not be a dripping faucet; help us to appreciate constructive criticism. Allow the words that are needed in our lives to refine and restore us to the luster that You intend for our lives. Lord God, Your Word lets us know daily that as we keep our eyes upon Your precepts, that the way of the wise is the way of true life. Our wisdom is not our own but divinely provided by You, and we are so thankful.

Dear Jesus, allow Your glory to overshadow any brokenness that we may feel. We ask that You cover the countenance of anyone who feels ashamed and unloved. Help Your vessels who read this prayer to know that they have been divinely selected as Your faithful servant to bring glory and honor to You as King of kings. Lord, we praise You, for You are worthy to be praised; and we thank You for Your grace and goodness toward us.

This is Your Chosen Vessels prayer, and we are waiting for the refining that Your Word will bring us. It is in Your Son, Jesus' name that we decree and declare healing, restoration, and salvation to our family and friends. Amen!

What has God revealed to you as you meditate on the scripture?

____

____

____

____

____

____

____

____

____

____

_____________________________________ *Journal*

QUESTIONS TO PONDER

Wisdom is Like a Life-Giving Fountain

1. How is wise counsel like a life-giving fountain?
2. Do you apply the principles of wise counsel and think before you act?
3. Are you willing to persevere and go the distance as a wise messenger who uses good sense for God?

What is your prayer today?

Journal

PRAYER THEME

Wise Women Fear the Lord

Prayer Focus: Proverbs 14:1-3, NKJV

The wise woman builds her house, But the foolish pulls it down with her hands. He who walks in his uprightness fears the LORD, But *he who is* perverse in his ways despises Him. In the mouth of a fool *is* a rod of pride, But the lips of the wise will preserve them.

Prayer Focus Reflection

His love is always with us and our God is right beside us. As we sit at the feet of our Lord and begin to worship Him in spirit and in truth, let us reflect on Proverbs 14:1-3.

This passage of Scripture teaches us that the woman in this text is wise because she reverences as well as fears the Lord. A wise woman thrives because she understands that wisdom offers her prosperity and happiness for her family. This wise woman cares for her family and can discern between what is wise and what is foolish. Wisdom separates the foolish woman from the wise woman, because the wise woman understands the benefits of wise decision making. She applies wisdom to every decision she makes about her relationships.

Let us ask God to help us to apply wisdom to our decision making:

Abba, we come to You this day to reflect on Your Word spoken in Proverbs 14:1-4. Lord, we ask You to help us make wise choices in everyday matters. We know that all we need to do is to bring every thought unto You and cast our cares upon You, for You care for us (1 Peter 3:5). Guide us in our daily lives and order our steps that they may align with Your perfect way and path.

Lord, we surrender our feelings of being overwhelmed and ask You to help us achieve balance. Help us to let our yes be yes and our no be no without shame or frustration. Let us lean not to our own understandings but help us to yield to Your promptings and the teaching that You have outlined for us.

We are grateful for Your Word and Your way. It is in the name of Jesus that we decree and declare healing in our minds, bodies, and souls. Lord Jesus, we thank You, O King of kings, for hearing our cry on this day. We also thank You for teaching us to have the best yes!

What has God revealed to you as you meditate on the scripture?

____

____

____

____

____

____

____

____

________________________________ *Journal*

QUESTIONS TO PONDER

Wise Women Fear the Lord

1. Have you considered the wise principles that aid in your family prospering?
2. What are some wise nuggets from which the Lord wants you to benefit in fearing Him as your Lord?
3. Are you willing to align your steps and walk uprightly?

What is your prayer today?

Journal

PRAYER THEME

Crowned with Knowledge

Prayer Focus: Proverbs 14:18, NKJV

The simple inherit folly, But the prudent are crowned with knowledge.

A Prayer of Reflection

Today is Your day, Lord, and we rejoice in it. You have given us another opportunity to be at Your gate and to call on Your mighty name. Lord God, creator of the universe, allow Your Chosen Vessels to be accountable to one another and help us to lean not to our own understanding. Help us to not be simpletons, but to be wise stewards in all that we do. Help us, Lord, to use the wisdom that You have bestowed upon us and walk the predetermined steps by Your righteousness.

Lord, some of us have made decisions that have plagued our minds and yielded a lack of forgiveness in our hearts; we ask You to forgive us and help us to forgive others. Teach us daily through Your Word to surrender our thoughts and fears unto You. Keep us, Lord, and guide us to no longer have clouded judgement; crown us with Your knowledge and grace so we can be wise women who walk in good judgement in all that we do.

Father help us to be more accountable in our daily walk. We ask You to surround us with Your grace. Let each day have a corporate focus on things that are pure, holy, and of a good report. Thank You for helping our sisters whose hearts, minds, and souls are weak and hurting. Lord, restore each of us, mend the brokenhearted, and mend the minds that are feeling bouts of depression and hopelessness. God remove any restlessness and allow a peace to surpass all understanding in each of us. Let us forever remember that You are with us and that You will never leave us nor forsake us. Father, we stand on Proverbs 14:18b that speaks of how the wise, sensible person is crowned with knowledge. Help us, Lord, to be sensible people of strong faith. Thank You for breaking the chains and restoring us to a proper place in You, dear God.

This is our prayer, and we give You all the glory and the praise. It is in Your name, Jesus, that we pray and give thanks. Amen.

What has God revealed to you as you meditate on the scripture?

Journal

QUESTIONS TO PONDER

Crowned Knowledge

1. Has your mind been plagued with unforgiveness?
2. What are some things you need to confess that have clouded your judgement?
3. Are you willing to break the chain of unforgiveness and receive a crown of knowledge?

What is your prayer today?

Journal

PRAYER THEME

Become Wise Not Foolish

Prayer Focus: Proverbs 14:31-33, NKJV

He who oppresses the poor reproaches his Maker, But he who honors Him has mercy on the needy. The wicked is banished in his wickedness, But the righteous has a refuge in his death. Wisdom rests in the heart of him who has understanding, But *what is* in the heart of fools is made known.

Prayer Focus Reflection

Our "spiritual vitamins" today come from Proverbs 14:31-35. In this passage of Scripture, God's Word describes the godly as one who honors, has mercy, is hopeful, walks in wisdom, and has understanding. We should willingly exalt the nation, and note that God, the King, grants favor toward wise servants. The opposite is true for the wicked. The wicked oppress the poor, are lured away by wickedness, walk in foolishness, abide in sin, and receive wrath from the King, who causes shame.

Let us pray for discernment:

Father, this is Your day. We come on behalf of the simple, those who cannot tell the difference between Your truth and falsehood. Help us, Lord, to show love and shower loving kindness on all we meet. We ask,

Lord, that all the simple hear Your Word and turn their hearts toward Your wisdom. Lord God, we stand in the gap of the scornful and ask that You bridge the path of the scoffed, those who laugh at Your wisdom. Forgive, Lord, all us and our loved ones who traveled this pathway. Help us, dear Lord, to no longer toy with wickedness. Lead us toward the wisdom and grace that awaits us. Abba, sometimes we tread in arrogance and foolishness because we lean to our own understanding and willingly ignore Your wisdom without any intention to abide by Your knowledge outlined in the Holy Scripture. Again, we ask for Your forgiveness.

Jehovah-Jireh, God our provider, we commit to be better stewards who read, study and pray Your Word.

Jehovah-Nissi, deliver us from complacency and guide us, dear Lord, to seek daily to obtain wisdom from Your Word and the wise counsel that You have set amongst us in this journey of life.

Jehovah-Shalom, Prince of peace, sometimes we walk in a state of rebellion, which we know is foolish. We have hated to fall in line with the wisdom You set before us. Forgive us, Jesus. We do not want to reject Your wise counsel delivered to us through Scripture, through Your prophet, Your spokesperson, or a Chosen Vessel. Abba, we seek to exalt You and abide by Your understanding that You have deposited in the pages of Your Holy Word.

Elohim, All-Knowing God, we thank You for all that You have spoken to us this day and what you will speak in the days to come. We ask You to continue to speak life over all who feel depressed, rejected, and insecure. Help us all to see areas in our lives that need a gentle touch of wisdom. Oh Lord, our God, deliver us and let us daily strive to be wise servants fueled by Your love, O King of kings and Lord of lords. This is our prayer, Lord Jesus, amen.

QUESTIONS TO PONDER

Become Wise Not Foolish

1. How has God's wisdom rested in your heart?
2. Were you a person who shared God's loving kindness with all those you met today?
3. What were some steps you took today to be a better steward for the kingdom of God?

What is your prayer today?

Journal

Speak Wisely and Bridle the Tongue

Prayer Focus: Proverbs 15:1-3, NKJV

A soft answer turns away wrath, But a harsh word stirs up anger. The tongue of the wise uses knowledge rightly, But the mouth of fools pours forth foolishness. The eyes of the LORD *are* in every place, Keeping watch on the evil and the good.

A Prayer of Reflection

Today's prayer focus comes from Proverbs 15 and includes several themes and offers us God's perspective in these areas. These biblical "spiritual vitamins" help to build us up and grant us a passion to honor the Lord, for He is the Lord of our life. Wisdom was in the beginning, and wisdom will give us hope, peace, love, and joy.

God speaks in Proverbs 15:4 KJV that a wholesome tongue is a tree of life: but perverseness is a breach in the spirit. Our prayer today is that Lord will help our tongues to bring healing and not destruction. We can find happiness and have a merry heart when we apply wisdom at the onset. We understand from Scripture that a heart of righteousness seeks to study, and that if we do not plan, then our plans will fail due to a lack of good counsel. The Lord can tear down the prideful and help those in need.

When we reverence God, we honor Him. Humility is the platform that leads to honor. Our goal should be to walk in the spirit of humility to bring the Lord glory and honor, as shared in Proverbs 15:33.

Let us ask God to guard our tongues:

Father God, thank You for a heart of love for the Chosen Vessels. Thank You, God, for allowing the Holy Spirit to guide our hearts to study our thoughts before giving an answer. Thank You, Lord Jesus, for giving us a merry heart of love, joy, and peace to worship You and serve others. Please help us to bridle our tongues, so we may bring glory ton Your name. Lord, help us to allow our tongues to be a "tree of Life" and not a tree that brings death. Father, we want to thank You for Your words, wisdom, and instruction. These verses on wisdom in speech and the blessing of good advice represent life choices with spouses, families, friends, and foes.

Father, we thank You that Your eyes are everywhere, and we thank You for keeping watch and for Your love and guidance.

Father, we did not know Your words, or the proper approach to use wisdom and instruction before some of the earlier battles in our family homes. We thank You for Your wisdom and for teaching us how to deal with anger. Father, we continue to pray for Your guidance and wisdom for our daily walk. Help us to apply the principles found in Proverbs 15 and help us to walk in love, joy, peace, and happiness.

Father allow the past hurts and pains to be filled with Your love and grace. Lord, touch spouses who walk in pride and greed. Help them to experience deliverance and bring peace back to the family. Continue to allow the boundaries that have been set to reflect Your perfect will. Help each of us to grow deeper in Your Word. Father help our spouses who have strayed away return to the fold. Encourage our spouses and loved ones in the fold to remain there and keep each of us in Your perfect will today and in the days to come.

Father God, we bless You for allowing us to have a heart of righteousness because of our relationship to You. Thank You, dear Lord, for a period to work out the details in our lives as well as granting us time to think before we speak and helping us to pay attention to what comes out of our mouths. Father, we desire to speak and pour out good not evil.

Father, we thank You for Your awesome power and for bringing the rain over our lives. Our blessings have been abundant, and we know You have greater in store for us and for those who are in our lives. We exalt Your mighty name, for our fear of displeasing You is the impetus for our thoughts, words, and deeds. We seek only to please You, and we long to hear Your voice daily to provide us with guidance and instruction. We thank You for seasons of sacrifice and necessary pruning, for we know that You do it because You love us, and when accepted in humility, we grow in wisdom. We thank You, praise You, and honor You for enabling us to hear Wisdom's instruction and have good counsel surrounding us. It is in the matchless name of Jesus, the Christ, we pray. Amen.

QUESTIONS TO PONDER

Speak Wisely and Bridle the Tongue

1. What is the purpose of abiding by God's Word today and giving others a soft answer to avoid stirring up anger?
2. How has your unbridled tongue affected your relationships?
3. Are you willing to allow the Lord to bridle your tongue so you can have a wise tongue?

What is your prayer today?

Journal

PRAYER THEME

Commitment is Our Lifeline to Godly Living

Prayer Focus: Proverbs 16:1-3, NKJV

The preparations of the heart *belong* to man, But the answer of the tongue *is* from the LORD. All the ways of a man *are* pure in his own eyes, But the LORD weighs the spirits. Commit your works to the LORD, And your thoughts will be established.

Prayer Focus Reflection

God's Word is so awesome. When I think of the goodness of Jesus and all that He has done for so many of us, my soul cries out, "Hallelujah and thank you, God, for keeping, saving, delivering, restoring, and leading us." God meets us right where we were. Some of us experienced job and furlough fatigue, but God's Word is a lifeline to all those who obey and trust Him. Proverbs 9:10-11 says,

> Fear of the Lord is the beginning of wisdom. Knowledge of the Holy One results in understanding. Wisdom will multiply your days and add years to your life.

God speaks to those with an obedient heart and reminds us that He has the final word. This means no matter the circumstance, God had the final say!

Bless the Lord for His godly principles that prepare and enable us to flow in His anointing. Proverbs 16:3 gives us instruction to place our confidence regardless of job, furlough, fatigue, or any life challenges. Proverbs 16:3 directs us to commit our lives to godly living. Notice these different Bible versions of that verse:

- † Commit your works to the Lord, And Your thoughts will be established. (NKJV)
- † Commit your work to the Lord, and your plans will be established. (ESV)
- † Roll your works upon the Lord [commit and trust them wholly to Him; He will cause your thoughts to become agreeable to His will, and] so shall your plans be established and succeed. (Amplified)
- † Put God in charge of your work, then what you have planned will take place. (MSG)

The Scripture theme centers on us having a merry heart. In addition, God's Word says in Proverbs 16:23,

> The heart of the wise teaches his mouth and adds learning to his lips.

This passage of Scripture reminds us that, through praise and worship, we can experience wisdom in all our ways as we acknowledge our God. Our obedient hearts and walking in wisdom enable each of us to prepare our hearts and minds to experience the pure joy that God sets up for those who walk uprightly. We can experience His wisdom and walk in good judgment because of our relationship with the Lord and our seeking to have a godly character. Our merry heart and cheerful countenance enable us to have joy in the Lord who is our strength.

The Lord gives a wholesome tongue to those who are kind and gentle and puts away foolishness. Our Lord gives us wisdom, which blesses our life because He is a strong tower and He is our safety net, our provider, our shield, and our buckler. He is our strong tower; when we put our confidence and expectations in His hands, then He will show us how significantly Proverbs 16:22 speaks so clearly to us.

God's Word says, "Understanding is a wellspring (source of continual supply, *Merriam Webster Dictionary*) of life." Despite any tension or strained relationships with people due to places or things, our Lord gave us His Word to help us along our way. God's Word offers us peace that surpasses our understanding. Remember, "Understanding is a wellspring of life." Life reflects many things that can be good, bad, or indifferent; but we can have every confidence that God's Word enables us to stake our work and our lives on God and His way. God's Word speaks volumes. Look back at Proverbs 16:9, which says,

- † *A man's heart plans his way, But the Lord directs his steps. (NKJV)*
- † *A man's mind plans his way, but the Lord directs his steps and makes them sure. (AMP)*

Chosen Vessels, each day we are getting wiser and stronger by reading, praying, and studying God's Word! Let us daily walk according to the ordered steps of our Lord, for He knows the plans He has for us!

QUESTIONS TO PONDER

Commitment is Our Lifeline to Godly Living

1. How have you prepared or committed your heart to God today?
2. How has your commitment to God affected your relationships?
3. What are the building blocks of God's Word that allow your understanding to be a wellspring?

What is your prayer today?

Journal

PRAYER THEME

Having a Good Name for Moral Living

Prayer Focus: Proverbs 22:1-3, NKJV

A *good* name is to be chosen rather than great riches, Loving favor rather than silver and gold. The rich and the poor have this in common, The LORD *is* the maker of them all. A prudent *man* foresees evil and hides himself, But the simple pass on and are punished.

Prayer Focus Reflection

Today's lesson focuses on advice for moral living, which means "conforming to a standard of right behavior." So many people view our behavior daily to see how our lives reflect the character of our Lord. God has given us biblical principles to direct us throughout this journey of life. Bless the Lord for His godly principles that prepare and enable us to flow in His anointing. Proverbs 22:1 gives us instruction on how to live moral lives:

- † *A good name is to be chosen rather than great riches, Loving favor rather than silver and gold. (NKJV)*
- † *A sterling reputation is better than striking it rich; a gracious spirit is better than money in the bank. (MSG)*

Proverbs 22:4 says,

- † *By humility and the fear of the LORD Are riches and honor and life. (NKJV)*
- † *The payoff for meekness and Fear-of-GOD is plenty and honor and satisfying life. (MSG)*

The theme in this Proverb centers on us achieving excellence in all we do. Everything that we do should be done unto the Lord because God created the world in excellence. In Genesis 1:26-31, God created the fish of the sea, the birds of the air, and the beasts of the field. He created all the plant life. He created male and female and commanded them to be fruitful and multiply and fill the earth. Then in Genesis 1:31 we see,

> And God saw everything that He had made, and behold, it was very good (suitable, pleasant) and He approved it completely.

God taught us how to be diligent in our work. God equipped each of us with a unique gift that bears our own fingerprint, with specific skills and abilities that align with the intended purpose of our life. God is the head of the universe, and we should align our thoughts, work patterns, and godly duties with His divine purpose. Finally, let us render good service in all that we do to attract and win others to the kingdom. Everything we do is about kingdom building and sharing the gospel. Look at Proverbs 22:29, which says,

> Do you see a man who excels in his work? He will stand before kings; He will not stand before unknown men. (NKJV)

Chosen Vessels, let us daily walk according to the ordered steps of our Lord for He knows the plans He has for us throughout this journey of life.

QUESTIONS TO PONDER

Having a Good Name for Moral Living

1. Have you considered the purpose of having a good name?
2. Do your passions align with your good name?
3. Are you willing to persevere and go the distance no matter what in pursuing your divine purpose to give good service?

What is your prayer today?

Journal

PRAYER THEME

Subjecting to God-Given Discernment

Prayer Focus: Proverbs 29:1-3, NKJV

He who is often rebuked, *and* hardens *his* neck, Will suddenly be destroyed, and that without remedy. When the righteous are in authority, the people rejoice; But when a wicked *man* rules, the people groan. Whoever loves wisdom makes his father rejoice, But a companion of harlots wastes *his* wealth.

Prayer Focus Reflection

Today's lesson focuses on "How to Tell the Wise from the Foolish." Wisdom is defined as *the ability to discern inner qualities and relationships.* Spending time learning more about the wisdom of God and the value of using God-given discernment in speaking and living our lives helps us to discern God's principles for our lives.

The theme that seems to drip with God's anointing is that we are to trust God and subject our discernment to His principles. The following Scriptures outline a path that models good sense and good judgment that brings glory and honor to Abba Father. We learn from Scripture that the foolish people are quick to vent and defend, but a wise person understands the value of holding back. Proverbs 29:11-12 gives us some biblical instruction on how we can apply this principle:

> A fool vents all his feelings, But a wise man holds them back.
> If a ruler pays attention to lies, All his servants become wicked.
> (NKJV)

The biblical principles outlined in Proverbs 29:12 remind us that sometimes people cannot discern the truth from a lie. However, truth can prevail when we use God's gift of discernment. A wise person can discern truth by practicing humility. Having a gift of discernment enables us to focus on creating spaces that encourage and warrant truth. Your situation during this season offers you an opportunity to embrace a reward because you walk in truth. Take time each day to separate your wise thoughts from your foolish thoughts. Choose each day which path you will take by asking yourself whether you are going to walk a path of righteousness
or foolishness.

Today, instead of casting off the restraints of the law, let us cast off instead anything in our lives that would keep us from walking according to God's law. As Proverbs 29:18 says,

> Where there is no revelation, the people cast off restraint;
> But happy is he who keeps the law. (NKJV)

This passage of Scripture above is reminding us that God's Word offers us guidance. Those who do not yield to God's Word are foolish. Our desire, aim, and purpose should be to want the wisdom of God to control our lives. We want to commit daily to walk according to His anointing and fulfill His plan for the life He planned for us. So, let us come off any high mountain that does not elevate God. Let us recognize that God honors those who have a lowly spirit and walk in integrity and humility. Proverbs 29:23-25 (CEV) says,

> Too much pride brings disgrace; humility leads to honor. If you take part in a crime, you are your worst enemy, because even under oath you cannot tell the truth. Do not fall into the trap of being a coward—trust the Lord, and you will be safe.

As reflected in Scripture, today's theme centers on us abiding in God and trusting Him for our circumstances. Our need could be for a new job, the same job, or no job. God is our peace, and through His peace, He will guide us on this journey of life. I like what it says in Proverbs 29:11 (CEV),

> Do not be a fool and quickly lose your temper—be sensible and patient.

Therefore, Chosen Vessels, remember that the enemy will tell you the lie that you cannot make it, that you are not qualified, that you do not have a purpose; but the devil is a liar and the father of lies, and the truth is not in him. Your task is to remember Proverbs 29:18 (CEV), which says:

> Without guidance from God, law and order disappear, but God blesses everyone who obeys his Law. God equipped each of us with a unique gift that bears our own unique identity and specific skills and abilities that align with God's intended purpose for our lives. Remember, life is about kingdom building and sharing the Gospel of Jesus. God gave each of us a unique design and character for the purpose of winning others to the kingdom.

Chosen Vessels, each day as you read God's Word, as you pray God's Word, as you are a beacon of light for God, you are becoming wiser and stronger because of God's Word. Walk according to the ordered steps of our Lord, for He knows the plans He has for us. Chosen Vessels, determine whether you are walking in wisdom or foolishness, and remember that humility brings honor. As you know, God has the final say; we do not. If you are a person who just has to have the last word, step back and keep yourself under control. Just trust God.

What has God revealed to you as you meditate on the scripture?

Journal

QUESTIONS TO PONDER

Subjecting to God-Given Discernment

1. What is the purpose of having godly discernment?
2. Is passion needed to share with others your unique gifts that bear your own fingerprint?
3. Are you willing to persevere and go the distance no matter what if you cannot have the last word?

What is your prayer today?

Journal

PRAYER THEME

Tabletop Wisdom

Prayer Focus: Proverbs 31:15, 17, and 28, NKJV

She also rises while it is yet night, And provides food for her household, And a portion for her maidservants…She girds herself with strength, and strengthens her arms…Her children rise up and call her blessed; Her husband also, and he praises her:

Prayer Focus Reflection

God's power, God's steadfast love, and God's grace are present in our lives! Proverbs gives each Chosen Vessel a biblical message on wisdom. What we get from God's Word will revive our hearts, minds, and souls for God's purpose. Let us take some time to allow this passage of Scripture to speak life and serve as a testament of instructions to apply wisdom to our daily lives. Think of your life like a table, and ask yourself these questions: 1) What is on your table? 2) What do you need to set before the Lord on that table?

Place Settings: ***Wisdom, Satisfaction, Strength, and Peace***

Centerpiece: ***Happiness***

The first-place setting is **WISDOM**. Pray for God's wisdom to help you through all situations in life. Allow His wisdom to prevail in all your relationships and help you make better and wiser decisions with finances and health.

The second-place setting is ***SATISFACTION***. Pray that you can accept and be satisfied with yourself and how God made you. Pray to accept what you cannot change as well as be satisfied with what He has supplied and given you. He knows what is best for each of us.

The third-place setting is ***STRENGTH***. Pray for the strength to persevere and keep pressing on. Even when times seem difficult, when the problems seem like they will never end, recognize that you get strength as you keep pressing on and doing what needs to be done for your family and being a good example. Ask God for the strength to teach those over whom you have stewardship. Ask God to guide those under your leadership. Seek God for the right approach to discipline, love and protect your loved ones.

The fourth-place setting is ***PEACE***. Pray for peace and happiness for marriages and all relationships. Peace keeps away anger, stress, worrying and fighting. Daily pray for healing and restoration. The Serenity prayer comes to mind. Take some time today to pray a serenity prayer.

We place ***HAPPINESS*** as a centerpiece on our table. God has given us unconditional love, joy, grace, and mercy. He provides protection and strength during times when we feel weak and sad. Just thinking of how awesome God is should make us happy. Proverbs 30:5 tells us that every word of God is pure and that He is a shield to those who put their trust in Him. A shield is a covering, a protection—and God is our protection.

Let Us Corporately Pray the Proverbs:

Father God, thank You for allowing us to have illustrations of Your Word. We do not always understand, but we know that You know what we need in order to ponder and chew on Your Word daily. Father, we thank You for the words shared and that each of us have what we need at our table. Dear Lord, we beseech You for mercy for all our unsaved loved ones. We ask that You help them to surrender unto Your way and that as they go through life's journey that they not harden their hearts. Make them receptive to Your will and way.

Lord, we ask that You keep us faithful as we commit to celebrate Your bringing our sons and daughters to the fold and returning them to their rightful place in You. We are so thankful that You have given us Your bread of life, so we may share with others. Lord, we are excited about every aspect of our life, be it little like the ant or loud as the lion's roar. Help us to continue to chew on Your grace and set boundaries to surround all those we love with Your love, grace, joy, and peace.

Lord, help us to be honest if we have placed the wrong things on our table, and help us to ask specific requests about what is needed in our lives. Let us seek You for understanding. As the eagle flies high to the mountaintop to preen, let us ask God to help us do the same. As the ant prepares in the summer for latter rain, let us prepare for those seasons of lack. Help us, Lord, to be wise and not foolish. Help us to take the food that You supplied in Your Word and feast on it. Let us thank You daily for our daily bread. Let us learn from the badger and the Proverbs 31 woman the importance of building and securing our households. Help us to be like the locust and become united as vessels for Your purpose. Help us to be as skillful as the lizard and know that Your Word can ease us out of seen and unseen danger. Help us learn the value of wisdom and the benefits that are set before us. Thank You, Lord, for making available to us Your love, grace, peace, strength, protection, purpose, vision, hope, salvation, and continued support. Thank You for setting wisdom on each of our tables and giving us a heart of love as Your Chosen Vessels. Thank You, God, for teaching us the value of having wisdom for our daily walk on earth.

Lord, we honor You and thank You for enabling us to hear Wisdom's instruction, so we can be the wise vessels who are choosing to yield to Your sound advice for teaching those You called us to mentor this season and in the seasons to come.

Father God, may we continue to meditate on Your words and speak boldly of Your greatness so that we can lead all those with a hardened heart to Your Grace. Help us be respectful to You every day. Thank You, Abba, for giving unto us Your only begotten Son, Jesus Christ, as our Lord and Savior, Amen.

What has God revealed to you as you meditate on the scripture?

Journal

QUESTIONS TO PONDER

Tabletop Wisdom

1. What is the purpose of setting your table with wisdom?
2. Is there a difference between being passionate and being wise?
3. Are you willing to persevere and go the distance no matter what?

What is your prayer today?

Journal

AFTERWORD

Chosen Vessels, I wrote this book in hopes that you will continue to spend time with the Lord and gather in the morning, at noon, or in the evening to pray as well as journal what He speaks to you. No matter when you pick up this prayer devotional, the Lord has something for you to reflect on as He takes you into a deeper relationship with Him. Take the plunge, seek God, and spend time in prayer. Journal your thoughts and join in the prayer movement. Please remember my acronym for prayer.

Purpose

Revealed

Always *when you*

Yield to the everlasting Father *and*

Establish *a*

Relationship with *Him, our Lord, Savior, and God.*

Remember, Chosen Vessels pray daily and relationships matter to God!

For more information on *Chosen Vessels Pray with Purpose and Passion*, visit **www.giftedpublishing.com.** You can contact Maria E. White via email at **giftedpublishing2020@gmail.com**, via Twitter **@SisterReRe36**, or via Facebook **Maria Stamps White**.

ABOUT THE AUTHOR

Maria E. White is dedicated to serving women and teaching them the Word of God. She's a wife, mother, grandmother, woman of prayer, facilitator, intercessor, speaker, and teacher. She serves faithfully in women's ministry as a director of a wives' support ministry, a facilitator for a spiritual boot camp, facilitates online book studies on marriage, a women's conference speaker on topics such as prayer, marriage, communication, and a host of other topics to equip women to be the best version of themselves as God's chosen vessels.

In her spare time, she is engaging in conversations with daily family Zoom calls, actively involved with her church's women's group where she volunteers her spiritual gifts, time, and talents. Maria lives in the Washington Metropolitan Area where her first ministry lies with being a wife to her husband for more than 30 years, a mom to two sons, one daughter-in-love, one grandson, and a spiritual mother as well as a mentor to many.

ISBN: 978-1-7358977-0-7

CPSIA information can be obtained
at www.ICGtesting.com
Printed in the USA
BVHW042019310721
612470BV00004B/9